THE BEST
STAGE SCENES
FOR WOMEN
FROM THE 1980'S

JOCELYN A. BEARD has edited <u>The Best Men's Stage Monologues of 1990</u> and <u>The Best Women's Stage Monologues of 1990</u> (Smith and Kraus, Inc., 1991). She has also co-edited <u>Contemporary Movie Monologues: A Sourcebook for Actors</u> (Fawcett/Columbine, Spring 1991).

KRISTIN GRAHAM is a faculty member at Southern Connecticut State University where she teaches theater history and acting. She belongs to the Theatre Artists Workshop of Westport, Connecticut. She co-edited <u>Monologues from Literature: A Sourcebook for Actors</u> (Fawcett/Columbine, 1990).

ROBYN GOODMAN is an actress and co-Artistic Director with Carole Rothman of Second Stage Theatre in New York City.

D1413146

i

Other Books for Actors from Smith and Kraus

The Best Men's Stage Monologues of 1990
edited by Jocelyn Beard

The Best Women's Stage Monologues of 1990
edited by Jocelyn Beard

Street Talk: Character Monologues for Actors
by Glenn Alterman

Great Scenes for Young Actors from the Stage
Craig Slaight and Jack Sharrar, editors

The Best Stage Scenes for Men from the 1980's
edited by Jocelyn A. Beard and Kristin Graham

One Hundred Men's Stage Monologues from the 1980's
edited by Jocelyn A. Beard

One Hundred Women's Stage Monologues from the 1980's
edited by Jocelyn A. Beard

THE BEST
STAGE SCENES
FOR WOMEN
FROM THE 1980'S

Edited by
Jocelyn A. Beard
and
Kristin Graham

SK
A Smith and Kraus Book

A Smith and Kraus Book
Published by Smith and Kraus, Inc.

Cover design by David Wise
Text design by Jeannette Champagne

Manufactured on recycled paper in the United States of America

First Edition: June 1991
10 9 8 7 6 5 4 3 2

Publisher's Cataloging in Publication
(Prepared by Quality Books Inc.)

The Best stage scenes for women from the 1980's / edited by Jocelyn A. Beard and Kristin Graham. --
  p. cm.
  Includes bibliographical references.
  ISBN 0-962722-7-2
  1. Acting. 2. Drama--Collections. I. Beard, Jocelyn A., 1955-
II. Graham, Kristin, 1951-

PN2080   808.82
                    91-60868

Smith and Kraus, Inc.
Main Street, P.O. Box 10, Newbury, Vermont 05051
(802) 866-5423

ACKNOWLEDGMENTS

Grateful thanks to the playwrights for making this book possible.
Jocelyn A. Beard would also like to thank Sean Bagley and Melette
Moffat for their help with this project.

CONTENTS

CONTENTS

CONTENTS

FOREWORD

The ever-changing nature of human relationships provides fascinating inspiration for playwrights as can be seen in the revelations—sometimes painful, sometimes joyous—occurring between two characters in a well-crafted scene.

Just when we thought that the changing role of women in society had been chronicled to within an inch of its life, along came yet another decade and another host of challenges—both societal and personal—illustrating that women, like men, will never exhaust their realm of possibilities. Bold women daring to be unconventional in a world dominated by convention like Lettice and Lotte who fight loneliness by reenacting historical executions in Peter Shaffer's *Lettice & Lovage*; and Samm-Art Williams' indomitable Laura, a woman fighting to save her farm in *Woman from the Town* are just some of the characters that you will discover within these pages.

The scenes in this book, including scenes for two women as well as for one woman and one man, have been selected with every effort to provide actors with a wide range of characters, situations and moods; and it is my hope that by rehearsing and performing these scenes you will gain new and invaluable insight into the complexities of the human heart.

—Jocelyn A. Beard
Patterson, NY
April, 1991

INTRODUCTION

I wanted to be an actress from the age of four when my parents took me to see my first Broadway play. Thus began my quest for material appropriate to my wealth of emotional experience. Feverishly I performed nursery rhymes, Ogden Nash poems and excerpts from every musical comedy record worn thin from my oral memorization technique. My sister's friends would howl with laughter when I would don my top hat and cane and suavely perform my eight year old version of "I Have Often Walked Down This Street Before." At thirteen I was Anna Christie, at fourteen Blanche DeBois and finally at sixteen I wowed a group of community theatre directors with my tragic interpretation of Linda Loman's farewell speech in *Death of a Salesman*.

At seventeen I had run out of roles to play. Where were my mentors? Where were the books that could expose me to parts within my ken? Sadly, nowhere.

Jocelyn Beard and Kristin Graham have filled this void by compiling an excellent assortment of scenes for women from the 80's. This book is a treat. It's like a sampler of many delicious flavors that hopefully will whet your appetite to experience a whole body of contemporary literature.

While absorbing the issues of this frenetic decade, you can apply yourself to the different forms and styles contained in each playwright's work. Use this book as an invaluable resource. And unlike me, you will never run out of roles to play.

—Robyn Goodman
Co-Artistic Director
Second Stage Theatre

THE BEST
STAGE SCENES
FOR WOMEN
FROM THE 1980'S

SECTION I

One Man and One Woman

BACK STREET MAMMY
by Trish Cooke
London - Present - Skolar (40-50) - Maria (40-50)

Skolar - A West Indian patriarch
Maria - Skolar's long-suffering wife

Skolar has moved his family to England from the West Indies in hopes of making a better life for them. Many years later, his youngest child has begun dating, and Skolar finds it difficult to let go as can be seen in the following argument with his stalwart wife, Maria

MARIA: (singing). Avé Avé Avé Maria
mm mm mm mm mm mm mm mm *(Humming tune.)*
Emaculet Mayray
Arr hats arr on fiarr
mm mm mm mm mm mm mm mmm mm mm mm
SKOLAR: Woman stop dat blasted noise in me head.
MARIA *(louder)*: Avé Avé Arrrvay Ma ree aaah Avé Avé...
SKOLAR: Shot your mout!
(MARIA stops mid song, shuts her eyes, then begins the tune again.)
SKOLAR: I tell you to stop wid dat dam noise in me head dis morning you know...
MARIA: Wait wait a minute. Since morning you get up your face humph humph, like is something you want to say but you don't want to say it. Is what on you min' Skolar?
SKOLAR: Jus' don't sing no church song, I don't want to hear no church song. *(Pause.)* You don't hear de time your daughter come in my house las' night.
MARIA: Oh, is dat you want to say.
SKOLAR: Think I was sleeping? Think is only you alone care what time she in street.
MARIA: Is street you worry for? *(She laughs. She sings more militant.)* Em-ac-u-let May-ray
Ar-hats arr on fi-a—
SKOLAR: Woman I say Shot op!

1

BACK STREET MAMMY

MARIA: Is street you worry for Skol? Is really street you does put your min' on when you turn turn in you bed at night eh? Is really street?

(He hits her. She hits him back. He hits her again.)

MARIA: You think I never see you when you hear de car stop outside? Stan' up like a fool fool holdin' on to you pyjama. Why you hol' it so tight? You 'fraid it gonna drop. You forget is *me* you wife and I see it all before. Why you was spying on de children Skol? You jealous of de man? Eh Skol? You useless... You ol' man...

SKOLAR: No man going touch my daughter... No kiss me arse dirty... Not my girl no...

MARIA: Hear yourself. You is a sick ol' man Skol.

SKOLAR: Becasue I love my kids I sick?

MARIA: There's love and love. And de way you shame your daughters is a sick ol' man love.

SKOLAR: Is you de one dat jealous. Whappen Jacko don't visit you no more.

MARIA: Same ol' story eh Skol? Jus' can't let it res'. When is time for us to enjoy life togedder, look how we does jus' hurt one anodder. And it hurt you to think of me and Jacko enn it? Good. I glad it hurt you, you hear. I glad. Because you does hurt me too. Everyday I wake up you hurt me. Every day I see where I still is you hurt me. Every day you hear? I did have a life too, you know. I did use to want things too. I was a person too. I did use to want more but now I don't want any more. I can't stan' any more. I tired. So, is you is de man me true? And is you Skol, *you* I follow Inglan wid me big belly so you tell me where we go now. Two ol' people fightin', calling an ol' story to make de time go. Well go on Mr Skolar I right behind you, Maria gonna follow. You is de man and I is you dog... I is you dog...

SKOLAR: I going... I going for a drink.

BESIDE HERSELF
by Joe Pintauro
Island off New England - Present - Mary (55) - Harry (50s)

Mary - A woman living alone
Harry - A UPS Man

Mary is a woman living alone on a sparsely populated island with nothing but memories to keep her company. Occasionaly UPS deliveries serve to break the monotony of her life and here Mary bids adieu to Harry, the UPS driver, who is retiring.

(A freshly baked peach pie is cooling on MARY's kitchen table next to her poetry notebook. We hear the sound of a truck zooming by, so close that the maple leaves of the sucklings press against her screens. The frothy white confirmation dress is popping out of the opened zipper of the garment bag. MARY is singing Paper Moon to herself:)
MARY: ...but it wouldn't be make believe if you believed in me. *(She's happy to hear a truck slowing down. Truck door slams.)*
HARRY: *(Knock)* U.P.S.
MARY: Just come in.
HARRY: U.P.S.
MARY: *(Starting down the ladder with her boxes)* I said come in, Harry.
HARRY: Mrs. Candee?
MARY: I've got my hands all dusty, Harry. *(She brings the boxes forward, laying them near the chaise, next to other boxes that she put out earlier. These boxes contain her old purses, compacts, books, records, junk of the past that will come into play.)*
HARRY: You got a dead raccoon on the highway...
MARY: Yeah. Since yesterday.
HARRY: Pretty flattened out.
MARY: Uh, put the package anywhere. It's my fireproof kitchen curtains from Sears. Forgive the mess. My first September not back to teaching so I'm cleaning out my closets.
HARRY: I don't have no package, Ma'am. The storm last night...
MARY: *(Appreciatively)* Aw...you stopped by anyway.

3

BESIDE HERSELF

HARRY: Just to say goodbye.

MARY: Noooo.

HARRY: I have to retire. I'm retiring.

MARY: You, too?

HARRY: My wife is going to die. We're pulling the plug tomorrow.

MARY: What? Well, the pie's all cooled. Sit and have a slice.

HARRY: No. I have others to say goodbye to.

MARY: *(Hurt)* Oh, I see. *(Tip)* Well, you sit anyway. *(Cutting his piece of pie)* I decided to be nice to somebody for the first time in years and you're not going to spoil that chance. *(He sinks into a chair before the pie. The man is distraught and looking for comfort. He doesn't want her pie or her money.)* Are you from the mainland, Harry? I never asked.

HARRY: I couldn't live on this dark island. My life is tough enough.

MARY: How old was she?

HARRY: Is.

MARY: I mean...how old is she? Sorry.

HARRY: Forty-six.

MARY: Younger than me. What does she have?

HARRY: A brain tumor.

MARY: Tsk tsk tsk.

HARRY: She's been on life support, lung machine, and I.V. four months. Never made out a living will, you know? I got a court order yesterday. Got it yesterday. She didn't want to live, my wife.

MARY: Who would?

HARRY: Even before she got sick.

MARY: Huh? Sometimes there just isn't anything left.

HARRY: That's crazy.

MARY: What is there?

HARRY: What? To be healthy. To...bake a pie, to greet a friend....

MARY: To give them a tip and say goodbye.

HARRY: Never took a tip in my life. What I'm doin' is passing these out to my customers. *(He hands her a bracelet.)*

MARY: A bracelet?

HARRY: Uh...read. Now I'm not forcin' these on people.

4

BESIDE HERSELF

MARY: *(Reads from bracelet.)* Do...not...resuscitate.

HARRY: Why suffer needlessly?

MARY: Harry, you've brightened my day. Let me pay you for this. *(MARY goes to canisters and pulls out a roll of bills.)*

HARRY: It's a gift.

MARY: Then this is a gift. *(She hands it to him. He takes it.)*

HARRY: I'm not a beggar. *(Again a truck zooms by, filling the house with noise. HARRY awkwardly holds his tip. He hasn't touched the pie.)* My that highway noise comes right in here.

MARY: Have to call the police three times a week to scrape up the run-over animals.

HARRY: It's the moisture from the bog. Smokes up your windshield. I hit a little otter once. I didn't mean to...

MARY: They're run over all day long, over and over. Used to shovel them up to help 'em keep their dignity but I can't bear to look at them anymore. The squirrels... It's the snakes that just...break your heart, tire marks, ugh...lying limp on your shovel. It's like seeing God in his underwear. Then the turtles...shells crushed and that yellow stuff all over... *(Suddenly entranced and staring off)* Maybe I'm tired of living here.

HARRY: Now you've brightened my day.

MARY: Touché Harry. *(She starts to laugh.)*

HARRY: What are you laughing at?

MARY: You...you've been delivering here for how long?

HARRY: Twenty years.

MARY: Twenty years. I decide to bake you a pie and you disappear. The kiss of death without the thrill.

HARRY: Well, Mrs. Candee. I enjoyed...the years.

MARY: Goodbye, Harry. Think of me.

LA CHUNGA
by Mario Vargas Llosa
translated by David Graham-Young
A bar in Piura, Peru - 1945 - Lituma (30's) - Meche (20's)

Lituma - A gambler
Meche - A naive young prostitute

Lituma is a gambler who professes his undying love for Meche,
a young prostitute "belonging" to his friend. Meche is surprised
by his confession and the two discuss a way for her to leave her
pimp so that they may run away together.

MECHE: *(Surprised)* So it was you. The last person I would have
suspected. Mono or José, perhaps—they're always flirting with me, and
they sometimes go even further when Josefino isn't looking. But you,
Lituma, you've never said a single word to me.

LITUMA: *(Deeply embarrassed)* I've never dared, Mechita. I've
never quite been able to show what I felt about you. But, but I ...

MECHE: *(Amused at his awkwardness)* You're all sweaty, your voice
is trembling, you're so shy, it's painful. How funny you are, Lituma.

LITUMA: *(Imploring)* Please, don't laugh at me, Meche. For the
love of God... I beg you...

MECHE: Have you always been frightened of women?

LITUMA: *(Very sorrowfully)* Not frightened exactly. It's just that...
I never know what to say to them. I'm not like the others. When they
meet a girl they know how to chat her up, and make a date with her.
I've never been able to do that. I get so worked up, I can't get the
words out.

MECHE; Haven't you ever had a girlfriend?

LITUMA: I've never had a woman without paying for her, Mechita.
Only the whores at the Casa Verde. And they always make me pay.

MECHE: Just like you're paying for me now.

LITUMA: *(Kneeling before MECHE)* Don't compare yourself with
those whores, Mechita, not even in fun.

MECHE: What are you doing?

LITUMA: I'd never make you go down on your knees to me, like
Josefino does. I'd spend my life on my knees in front of you. I'd

6

worship you, Meche, as if you were a queen. *(He crouches down and tries to kiss her feet.)*
MECHE: Ha ha, when you do that, you're just like a little lapdog.
LITUMA: *(Still trying to kiss her feet)* Then at least let me be your lapdog, Meche. I'll obey you, I'll be loving and gentle whenever you want or if you'd rather I'll just lie still. Don't laugh, I'm being serious.
MECHE: Would you really do anything for me?
LITUMA: Try me.
MECHE: Would you kill Josefino if I asked you to?
LITUMA: Yes.
MECHE: But I thought he was your friend.
LITUMA: You're worth more to me than any friend, Mechita. Do you believe that?
(MECHE puts her hand on his head, as if stroking an animal.)
MECHE: Come, and sit beside me. I don't want anyone to grovel to me like that.
LITUMA: *(Sitting beside her, on the bed, without daring to go very close to her or even touch her)* I've been in love with you since the first day I saw you. In the Río-Bar, on the Old Bridge. Don't you remember? No. Why should you remember? You never seemed to take any notice of me, even when you were looking straight at me.
MECHE: In the Río-Bar?
LITUMA: José, Mono and I were in the middle of a game, when in came Josefino with you on his arm. *(Imitating him)* Hey, look what I've found. What d'you think of her, eh? Then he lifted you up by the waist and paraded you in front of everyone. *(His face suddenly clouds over.)* I hate him when he does things like that to you.
MECHE: Does he make you jealous?
LITUMA: No, he makes me envious, though. *(Pause.)* Tell me, Mechita. Is it true he's got one this big? Is that why women are so crazy about him? He never stops bragging to us: 'Mine's a real whopper,' he says. But I've asked the whores in the Casa Verde and they say it's not true, that it's the normal size—just like everone else's.
MECHE: You aren't going to have much success with me if you say such disgusting things, Lituma.

7

LA CHUNGA

LITUMA: I'm sorry. You're right, I shouldn't have asked you that. But, doesn't it seem unfair? Josefino behaves so boorishly with women. He knocks them around, they fall in love with him, and when he's got them really hooked, he sends them out to whore for him. And in spite of that, he still gets the ones he wants. Yet someone like me, who's an honest, well-meaning, gentlemanly sort, who'd be prepared to treat any woman who loved him like precious china, never gets any attention at all. I ask you, is that fair?

MECHE: It may not be fair. But is anything in life fair?

LITUMA: Is it because I'm ugly that they don't pay any attention to me, Mechita?

MECHE: *(Making fun of him)* Here. Let me have a look at you. No, you're not that ugly, Lituma.

LITUMA: Please be serious with me. I'm telling you things I've never told anyone in my life before.

(MECHE looks at him for a moment mistrustfully.)

MECHE: Did you fall in love with me the first time you saw me?

LITUMA: *(nodding)* I didn't sleep all night. In the darkness, I kept seeing you. I thought you were the most beautiful woman I'd ever seen. I thought women like you only existed in the cinema. I worked myself up into such a state that I even cried, Mechita. I can't tell you how many nights I've lain awake, thinking about you.

MECHE; And you say you don't know how to talk to women. It's beautiful, what you're telling me.

(LITUMA puts his hand in his pocket and takes out a small photograph.)

LITUMA: Look. I always carry you around with me.

MECHE: Where did you get that photo from?

LITUMA: I stole it from Josefino. It's a bit faded—with all the kissing I've given it.

MECHE: *(Stroking his head again)* Why didn't you ever say anything to me before, silly?

LITUMA: We've still time, haven't we? Marry me, Mechita. Let's leave Piura. Let's start a new life.

MECHE: But you're broke, Lituma. Like the rest of the superstuds. And you've never done a day's work in your life, either.

LA CHUNGA

LITUMA: Because I've never had anyone to push me, to make me change the way I live. You don't think I enjoy being a superstud, do you? Marry me—you'll see how different I can be, Mechita. I'll work hard, I'll do anything. You'll always have everything you want.

MECHE: Would we go to Lima?

LITUMA: To Lima, yes. Or wherever you want.

MECHE: I've always wanted to go to Lima. It's such a large city, Josefino would never find us.

LITUMA: Of course not. And besides what would it matter if he did find us? Are you afraid of him?

MECHE: Yes.

LITUMA: With me you wouldn't be. He's quite harmless, really, he's just a loud mouth., I know him very well—we were kids together. He's not from round here, of course—he's from the Gallinacera. There, they're all talk and no action.

MECHE: Well, he's not all talk with me. He sometimes beats me practically unconscious. If I left him to go away with you, he'd kill me.

LITUMA: Nonsense, Meche. He'd get himself another woman, just like that. Let's go to Lima. Tonight.

MECHE: *(Tempted)* Tonight?

LITUMA: We'll catch the bus from the Cruz de Chalpón. Come on.

MECHE: Shall we get married?

LITUMA: As soon as we get to Lima, I promise you. It's the first thing we'll do. Would you like that? Shall we go? *(Pause.)*

MECHE: Let's go. We'll never return to Piura. I hope I won't live to regret this one day, Lituma.

LITUMA: *(Kneeling again)* I promise you never will, Mechita. Thank you, thank you. Ask me for something, anything you want, just tell me to do something.

MECHE: Get up, we've no time to waste. Go and pack your suitcase, and buy the tickets. Wait for me at the Cruz de Chalpón bus station. Halfway up Avenida Grau, all right? I'll be there, just before twelve.

LITUMA: Where are you going?

MECHE: I can't just leave without taking anything with me. I'm going to fetch my things. Just a few essentials.

LITUMA: I'll come with you.

MECHE: No, it's not necessary. Josefino is in the Casa Verde and he never gets back till dawn—I've got more than enough time. We mustn't be seen together on the street though, no one must suspect a thing.

LITUMA: *(Kissing her hands)* Mechita, Mechita, darling. I'm so happy I can't believe it's true. *(Crosses himself, looks at the sky.)* Thank you God, dear sweet God. From now on I'm going to be different, I'm going to stop being lazy—I'm going to stop gambling, living it up, lying... I swear to you...

MERCHE: *(Pushing him)* Come on, hurry up, we're wasting time, Lituma. Quickly, run...

LITUMA: Yes, yes, whatever you say, Mechita.

(He gets up hurriedly, rushes towards the staircase, but there he loses his impetus. He slows down—comes to a halt—and slowly returns to the gambling table, weary and sad. The superstuds do not notice him. Once again the central focus is on them, as they continue to gamble, swear and drink toasts to each other.)

CRIMES OF THE HEART
by Beth Henley
Mississippi - Present - Meg (30's) - Doc (30's)

Meg - A middle sister
Doc - Meg's ex-lover

Meg and Doc had a big romance before she ran off to Hollywood to pursue a singing career. She has returned home a failure and here tells Doc, who is now married, why she really ran away.

DOC: Hello, Meggy.

MEG: Well, Doc. Well, it's Doc.

DOC *(after a pause)*: You're home, Meggy.

MEG: Yeah, I've come home. I've come on home to see about Babe.

DOC: And how's Babe?

MEG: Oh, fine. Well, fair. She's fair. *(Doc nods.)* Hey, do you want a drink?

DOC: Whatcha got?

MEG: Bourbon.

DOC: Oh, don't tell me Lenny's stocking bourbon.

MEG: Well, no. I've been to the store. *(She gets him a glass and pours them each a drink. They click glasses.)*

MEG: So, how's your wife?

DOC: She's fine.

MEG: I hear ya got two kids.

DOC: Yeah. Yeah, I got two kids.

MEG: A boy and a girl.

DOC: That's right, Meggy, a boy and a girl.

MEG: That's what you always said you wanted, wasn't it? A boy and a girl.

DOC: Is that what I said?

MEG: I don't know. I thought it's what you said.

(They finish their drinks in silence.)

DOC: Whose cot?

MEG: Lenny's. She's taken to sleeping in the kitchen.

11

DOC: Ah. Where is Lenny?

MEG: She's in the upstairs room. I made her cry. Babe's up there seeing to her.

DOC: How'd you make her cry?

MEG: I don't know. Eating her birthday candy; talking on about her boyfriend from Memphis. I don't know. I'm upset about it. She's got a lot on her. Why can't I keep my mouth shut?

DOC: I don't know, Meggy. Maybe it's because you don't want to.

MEG: Maybe.

(They smile at each other. Meg pours each of them another drink.)

DOC: Well, it's been a long time.

MEG: It has been a long time.

DOC: Let's see—when was the last time we saw each other?

MEG: I can't quite recall.

DOC: Wasn't it in Biloxi?

MEG: Ah, Biloxi. I believe so.

DOC: And wasn't there a—a hurricane going on at the time?

MEG: Was there?

DOC: Yes, there was; one hell of a hurricane. Camille, I believe they called it. Hurricane Camille.

MEG: Yes, now I remember. It was a beautiful hurricane.

DOC: We had a time down there. We had quite a time. Drinking vodka, eating oysters on the half shell, dancing all night long. And the wind was blowing.

MEG: Oh, God, was it blowing.

DOC: Goddamn, was it blowing.

MEG: There never has been such a wind blowing.

DOC: Oh, God, Meggy. Oh, God.

MEG: I know, Doc. It was my fault to leave you. I was crazy. I thought I was choking. I felt choked!

DOC: I felt like a fool.

MEG: No.

DOC: I just kept on wondering why.

MEG: I don't know why... 'Cause I didn't want to care. I don't know. I did care, though. I did.

12

DOC *(after a pause)*: Ah, hell— *(He pours them both another drink.)* Are you still singing those sad songs?
MEG: No.
DOC: Why not?
MEG: I don't know, Doc. Things got worse for me. After a while, I just couldn't sing anymore. I tell you, I had one hell of a time over Christmas.
DOC: What do you mean?
MEG: I went nuts. I went insane. Ended up in L.A. County Hospital. Psychiatric ward.
DOC: Hell. Ah, hell, Meggy. What happened?
MEG: I don't really know. I couldn't sing anymore, so I lost my job. And I had a bad toothache. I had this incredibly painful toothache. For days I had it, but I wouldn't do anything about it. I just stayed inside my apartment. All I could do was sit around in chairs, chewing on my fingers. Then one afternoon I ran screaming out of the apartment with all my money and jewelry and valuables, and tried to stuff it all into one of those March of Dimes collection boxes. That was when they nabbed me. Sad story. Meg goes mad.
(Doc stares at her for a long moment. He pours them both another drink.)
DOC *(after quite a pause)*: There's a moon out.
MEG: Is there?
DOC: Wanna go take a ride in my truck and look out at the moon?
MEG: I don't know, Doc. I don't wanna start up. It'll be too hard if we start up.
DOC: Who says we're gonna start up? We're just gonna look at the moon. For one night just you and me are gonna go for a ride in the country and look out at the moon.
MEG: One night?
DOC: Right.
MEG: Look out at the moon?
DOC: You got it.
MEG: Well...all right. *(She gets up.)*
DOC: Better take your coat. *(He helps her into her coat.)* And the

bottle— *(He takes the bottle. Meg picks up the glasses.)* Forget the glasses—
MEG *(laughing)*: Yeah—forget the glasses. Forget the goddamn glasses.

ELLIOT LOVES
by Jules Feiffer
Chicago - 1980's - Joanna (30's) - Elliot (30's)

Joanna - A woman considering a new commitment after two divorces
Elliot - In love with Joanna, also divorced

Joanna and Elliot have been seeing each other for six weeks and the time has been idylic. Lost in one another, they have remained relatively free of their individual lives and have fallen very much in love. The bubble is about to burst, however, for it is time for Elliot to introduce Joanna to his friends at an informal party. Here, they argue on the way to the party and we can see that in six weeks they haven't learned that much about each other.

(Evening. The lobby of a chic Chicago apartment building on the Near North Side. A mirror, a bench, an elevator.)
JOANNA: Tell me again.
ELLIOT: They're just the guys, that's all. Nothing to be afraid of.
JOANNA: Bobby, Phil, and Leo.
ELLIOT: Larry.
JOANNA: Larry's the one who just got divorced. *(ELLIOT nods.)* Piece of cake.
ELLIOT: And Bobby is married to Vera, and Phil is separated.
JOANNA: Larry is the house painter.
ELLIOT: He owns a paint company. He makes the paint, he doesn't paint houses himself. He's a businessman. Optimum Paints.
JOANNA: Don't get upset.
ELLIOT: I'm not upset. They're waiting for us. We're late.
JOANNA: Elliot, it's only eight o'clock. Don't get carried away.
ELLIOT: You're the one who wanted to meet my friends.
JOANNA: Well, don't you think it's just about time?
ELLIOT: I love you, Joanna. *(Pause.)* Look, they already know you. I've done nothing but rave about you to them. You're not going in there as a stranger. They love you. *(Pause.)* What are you thinking?

15

ELLIOT LOVES

JOANNA: You look very nice. I'm so glad you picked that suit over the one I wanted. You look radically handsome in it.
ELLIOT: You look good enough to eat.
(They kiss.)
JOANNA: Larry is black?
ELLIOT: Bobby is black.
JOANNA: And he has a white girlfriend.
ELLIOT: They split up.
JOANNA: Is he here alone?
ELLIOT: He's here with his wife, Vera. This is their apartment. They live here.
JOANNA: His wife took him back?
ELLIOT: No one's supposed to know about this. I don't know what Vera knows.
JOANNA: She's white?
ELLIOT *(impatient)*: Joanna...Black. She's a supervisor at the telephone company.
JOANNA *(memorizing)*: House painter...telephone company. Who's the accountant then—Larry?
ELLIOT: Phil.
JOANNA: Then what's Larry? Is he the one who hates women?
ELLIOT: He doesn't hate them. He just got out of a lousy marriage.
JOANNA: He did something just awful to her, though?
ELLIOT: It's complicated...
JOANNA: He did something. Don't tell me. Isn't he the one who stole his wife's car when they split up and drove it off a cliff?
ELLIOT: That doesn't mean he hates women.
JOANNA: He hates cars?
ELLIOT: That's funny.
JOANNA: I say something funny and you tell me it's funny. Well, I know it's funny. Don't you think I know, Elliot? Is it always necessary to point it out to me?
ELLIOT: I'm sorry if I do that. Is it really important, I mean, to discuss this right now?
JOANNA: You don't laugh at my jokes, you identify them. You do

not ever laugh at me. It provokes me. I love you anyhow.

ELLIOT: I'm sorry. Don't worry about Larry. He's had a year of therapy since he drove the car off the cliff.

JOANNA: Piece of cake. I've drawn a blank on Phil. Is he the alcoholic?

ELLIOT: Phil may be an alcoholic. He's got it under control.

JOANNA: We all drink too much.

ELLIOT: Try not to drink so much around Phil. I don't mean just you. Me too.

JOANNA: Phil will have to take care of himself. Tonight I have my own problems.

ELLIOT: He's gotten very quiet. You have to get used to Phil.

JOANNA: Does Phil have a girlfriend? First tell me what he does.

ELLIOT: He's the accountant.

JOANNA: And Bobby's the one who works for *Playboy*. He's the one with the black wife, Violet.

ELLIOT: Vera is her name.

JOANNA: She works. She works for...

ELLIOT: AT&T.

JOANNA: I was going to say that. I have it together. How do I look?

ELLIOT: You know what I think.

JOANNA: Hair all right?

ELLIOT: Joanna, let's go. Please. I love you.

JOANNA: Don't get carried away.

ELLIOT: I'm not. I'm just a little...

JOANNA: I love your tie. Did I buy that for you? It looks very smart with that shirt. Your friends are going to think I don't live up to you.

ELLIOT *(beams)*: I think you look beautiful.

JOANNA: Did you see that story in the *Tribune* this morning? Mayor Sawyer—

ELLIOT: Which story?

JOANNA: I was about to tell you, Elliot.

ELLIOT: Can you tell me upstairs?

JOANNA: Now calm down. Mayor Sawyer was in his limo on his way to a meeting on the North Side, when he spotted an old lady being mugged—are you all right?

ELLIOT: I just think we should get upstairs.

JOANNA: Don't let it get to you. And he got out of his limo—

ELLIOT: Whose limo?

JOANNA: Mayor Sawyer.

ELLIOT: Why are we talking about Mayor Sawyer?

JOANNA: It was a story. I'm telling you this amusing story from today's *Tribune* in order to relax you.

ELLIOT: Can you tell me in the elevator?

JOANNA: For pity's sake, we're going! Don't be rude. May I finish? He breaks up the mugging. And the police come. And they ask him his name. No one knows who he is!

ELLIOT: Wouldn't you say it's rude to be twenty-five minutes late to a dinner?

JOANNA: Elliot, no one, not the old lady, the muggers, the police—no one recognized the Mayor. *(A long exchange of stares.)* Piece of cake. I just want to go over my notes.

ELLIOT: That's also funny—notes.

JOANNA: I'm not joking. *(Scans notes.)*

ELLIOT: What are those? Seriously, Joanna.

JOANNA: Don't get hot and bothered.

ELLIOT: What notes? Let me see!

HOANNA: Now don't let it get to you. It's nothing at all. Just little reminders of what you like to have me talk about: the drugstore story, the Marshall Field story, the day I ran away from the kids.

ELLIOT: Oh, Joanna...

JOANNA: Your friends, Phil and Bobby and Larry, should like these. *(Finishes with notes.)* Okay. I must say, I'm exhausted.

ELLIOT: You're making too much of this.

JOANNA: They'll take to me, won't they, Elliot?

ELLIOT: No, it'll be fine. Fine!

JOANNA: Because if they don't—

ELLIOT: Believe me, Joanna, we may have problems but this is not going to be one of them.

ELLIOT LOVES

JOANNA: What problems do we have?

ELLIOT: I just mean—

JOANNA: This is a fine time to bring up our problems.

ELLIOT: You're the one who's always telling me, "Don't let it get to you."

JOANNA: This time I believe *you* are the naive one.

ELLIONT: You may be right.

JOANNA: Stop humoring me! You are naive, Elliot. You believe everything I tell you—even when I'm lying—so how can I trust your assurances about your friends?

ELLIOT: You don't lie. About what?

JOANNA: You're not even curious. I take advantage of you, Elliot.

ELLIOT: Please. Not now.

JOANNA: You know when we go out to dinner and I insist that this time it's on me and then I never have enough money and you have to pay?

ELLIOT: It's funny. It's charming. So what?

JOANNA: I have the money. I carry two hundred dollars in my purse at all times. I don't want to spend it. You'll never want to see me again when you hear this: I hate to spend money. I never pay for anything if I can help it, not even when I lunch with my girlfriends. They're onto me. It embarrasses them so that they don't bring it up, but they know very well what a cheapskate I am. You never guessed?

ELLIOT: You'd pay for me if it was important.

JOANNA: I would never pay for you.

ELLIOT: You don't mean that.

JOANNA: I would rather die than pay for you. *(Pause.)* I will buy things only for my children. Are you upset?

ELLIOT: Joanna, we were supposed to be upstairs half an hour ago. Please, I beg you!

JOANNA: I'd move heaven and earth for my children. I save all my money for my children's future. None of us can be sure about the future. I can't predict mine, much less theirs. I must provide for them.

ELLIOT: I agree. It's perfectly understandable.

JOANNA: You don't know what it means to have children. It doesn't

mean I don't love you. How did you get to be so old and not have
children? It's very selfish of you, really. How did your wife let you
get away with it? Without children, there's no substance to life. I'm
sure that's why she left you.

ELLIOT: She left me for another man.

JOANNA: And now she has children.

ELLIOT: I want children, Joanna. I have always wanted children.

JOANNA: If you wanted a child, you'd have one by now!

ELLIOT: I'd want a child with you.

JOANNA: I don't want any more children.

ELLIOT: Then what are we *talking* about?

JOANNA: I'm trying to understand the kind of man you are. Are you
truly that selfish? I don't believe you are. What's the answer?

ELLIOT: Look, I love your children. You've said it yourself, how
much they like me.

JOANNA: It's easy for you. It's not the same. You're not a real
person until you're a parent. You're a shadow. You're one-
dimensional.

ELLIOT: How can you talk to me this way? I take care of you. I run
errands. I serve you.

JOANNA: Remember, I serve you too. I'd respect you more if you
didn't talk about it. I hate you for saying that.

ELLIOT: I can't stand you hating me, Joanna.

JOANNA: Calm down. It's not all that serious.

ELLIOT: How can we go up to my friends with you hating me? You
know how late we are? How can you have secrets if you love me?

JOANNA: I don't believe anyone's ever loved you before. I must
protect myself.

ELLIOT: This hurts.

JOANNA: Don't be vulnerable with me now, Elliot. It's unkind.

ELLIOT: I know tonight is a strain...

JOANNA: —it's going to be a very bad time with us if they don't like
me.

ELLIOT: Then the hell with'em!

JOANNA: We will have a hard time surviving it. Believe me. You

know these men a lifetime. For example, I have two friends whom you will meet—my two closest friends—
ELLIOT: Joanna—
JOANNA: Walter and Fay Derringer.
ELLIOT: You've told me about them.
JOANNA: Please bear with me. And they are always touching each other, Walter and Fay, in front of me.
ELLIOT: What are you saying? I don't touch you enough?
JOANNA: Don't anticipate me. You touch me just fine. I don't know why, two people when they come together, the rest of the world changes dimension. Is the rest of the world so intolerable that just because you've found one other person, a man you prefer to be with—
ELLIOT: Is this going to take long?
JOANNA: —and when an outsider, a friend, breaks into that equation, for example Fay and I, we have known each other forever. When we're yammering away, I can see, visually see Walter disappearing before my eyes. The way my father did when my mother and her sisters held court. As if a woman diminishes a man if she's not paying full attention. Which is why I'm afraid sometimes because we've been alone, truly alone, and now I'll meet your friends and the next step is you will meet mine and forgive me, Elliot, but I find this just a bit threatening. Is that crazy?
ELLOIT: But sooner or later, Joanna—
JOANNA: I know that! Forgive me, I'm demented. But I do have a point. I know I do. This changes everything.
ELLIOT: We have to meet each other's friends eventually.
JOANNA: I want to meet your family.
ELLIOT: I don't believe this is happening!
JOANNA: What do you want me to do?
ELLIOT: This wasn't my idea.
JOANNA: Let's stand'em up.
ELLIOT: Be reasonable.
JOANNA: I don't want to meet your friends, Elliot.
ELLIOT: What do you want me to do? What am I supposed to do?
JOANNA: I'm not ready. I'm not sure I want to be judged yet.

ELLIOT LOVES

ELLIOT: It's too late, Joanna.

JOANNA: *You* go on up.

ELLIOT: I'm sorry. This is my fault. I'm sorry. I shouldn't have rushed it. What will I tell them? What can I possibly say?

JOANNA: Don't say anything. Please don't say anything. Please don't tell them anything about me. Come home with me now, Elliot!

ELLIOT: I can't do this, Joanna.

JOANNA: I'm going home. What are you going to do?

(ELLIOT rings for the elevator. It opens and he steps in. The door closes on him.)

ELLIOT *(muffled)*: It's 22G!

JOANNA *(facing elevator)*: Piece of cake.

THE FILM SOCIETY
by Jon Robin Baitz
South Africa - 1970 - Terry (40's) - Nan (40's)

Terry Sinclair - A teacher at the Blenheim School for Boys
Nan Sinclair - Terry's wife, also a teacher

When Terry invites a black minister to speak at a school
function at this all-white private school, he is consequently fired
from his job. Bitter and angry, he takes his frustration with the
system out on his wife, Nan, who is trying desperately to hang
on to both her job and her marriage. Here, they argue about
their future.

*(NAN and TERRY's flat. That night. TERRY is sitting, quite still, in
his corner chair, as NAN is heard, letting herself in, holding a small
bag of groceries and a bag of chinese food.)*
TERRY: Well. Good. See me, sitting here? Like an odd and patient
breed of dog, oh? *(NAN braces herself, smiles.)*
NAN: A long and bad, stupid day, Terry. So we'll give it a rest, for
tonight, right?
TERRY: *(Pause. TERRY looks at the bag.)* They actually let you take
merchandise out of there? I mean, I have to shout for a lamb chop.
NAN: He's not so bad.
TERRY: He is a little Indian racist, and I don't think we should be
giving him our business.
NAN: *(As calm as TERRY)* ...And why now, suddenly?
TERRY: *(Shrugs, smiling.)* He wouldn't sell me my smokes.
NAN: *(Taking a package of cigarettes from the bag.)* As long as
there's a social context, for your boycott... *(Pause. She sighs and
crosses to him.)*
TERRY: There's no such thing as a social context. It's all just
chemical, you know. I've been wrong all along. It's all about
mommy, daddy, genes, and neurons or something.
NAN: I've brought Chinese.
TERRY: Chinese, what a joke. Honorary whites. I wonder, is that
all 60 billion of them or just the ones living here. And what on earth

23

would possess a Chinaman to come to South Africa, eh? So. What? Why so late? Watching a flick with old Jonathon? A musical? *(pause)*
NAN: Ah. I see.
TERRY: *(Laughs a bit.)* Ah? You see?
NAN: The 'ah' of recognition. As in 'Ah, he's just spent the day in some sort of rage.' *(Pause. TERRY nods.)*
TERRY: *(Looks at the bag of groceries, picks out a tin of tea.)* Please, must you buy this cheap kaffir tea? I mean, I don't expect, like, Fortnum's Russian Caravan, exactly, but something other than 'twin roses'. Something that gives one the illusion that there's something mysterious to look forward to.
NAN: What I should do, is stop myself, rather soon, if I were you, love. Don't you think?
TERRY: The bug is off the phone.
NAN: ...Really? How—how can you tell?
TERRY: 'Cause they shut the phone off. You never paid them. I actually like this kind of little ironic victory.
NAN: I'll have it on tomorrow.
TERRY: Needn't bother. It's only you, or Jonathon—stuttering.
NAN: *What* is *wrong*? *(pause)*
TERRY: Jackson was arrested.
NAN: What for?
TERRY: What for? What do you think? You couldn't possibly imagine him out agitating, could you? He was violating the pass-laws.
NAN: You...you got him out, Ter?
TERRY: *(Calm, but utterly exhausted.)* That was interesting. My family name still carries. I think of myself as some sort of pariah, an outcast? But do the Bantu Affairs Police know me? They're busy with their own usual array of murky, oblique affairs. So. I got dressed, very carefully, and I went down to their little corner of hell with its stench of burning rubber reality, and I said to the warrant officer, 'Listen mate, that is my bloody servant you've go there, and my servant has windows to wash, and toilets to clean, and a lot to learn, so just hand him over to me, and I'll smack him.' *(pause)* And there was this hesitation. The suspicion of my Afrikaaner brethren is boundless. So,

I stood there, and looked him in the eye, rather contemptuously, and addressed him in Afrikaans: 'Hey, bloke. My grandfather *ran* your lousy outfit. I deserve a bit of respect and a lot of lee-way'...and he nods. *(pause)* This man has never heard of Blenheim. *(pause)* And he hands me Jackson.

NAN: So—he's alright?

TERRY: Oh, fine.

NAN: Jesus, it's endless.

TERRY: Isn't it? Of course, you've just come from a 'long, bad, and stupid day' yourself.

NAN: Actually, I have come from a pretty shoddy bit of manipulation and humiliation, and it has left me feeling pretty stupid, so Christ knows, I don't need to walk in here and be insulted by you.

TERRY: *(Picks up letter from the table beside the chair.)* Please don't tell me about your lousy day at Blenheim and your humiliations. Please. Not now. *(pause)* Because I have just received a letter from Victor Frame offering a job at the Esquella Americana in Rio de Janeiro, and I can't take it, because we don't have enough money to get out!

NAN: Victor Frame? Let me see...

TERRY: Blenheim: Class of 61. Was on the cricket team when I was captain. Worshipped me.

NAN: Well, let's start again. Look. I've got a raise, so if we put some money away, we could go, in about six months... *(pause)*

TERRY: Oh please, you must be joking. What pack of lies did they feed you? A raise? It's impossible. They're on the verge of shutting down by now, and I did it to them.

NAN: Wait a second. I'm telling you, Jonathon's got me a raise. Look, we can get out, it's all you talk about, come on.

TERRY: Jonathon...got you...a raise. Something's wrong here, Nan. It doesn't make sense. Come on, you're smart, what do you mean? Have you seen the place? It looks like a Moorish ruin. Jonathon? Raise? What? He could show you a double feature, but a raise...it's a lie, it's one of those things they say... *(beat)* I mean, don't be naive.

NAN: No, no, no. You don't understand. It was a very specific transaction, Terry. He made me take on yachting in return for the raise.

TERRY: Yachting, oh now we're into sheer fantasy. Yachting my dear, you couldn't put up a spinacker if there was one sticking out your bum. Don't be absurd. These boys'd kill you out there! You want to end up floating face down in Durban harbour, with half the school dancing on the prow? It's a con job! Yachting.

NAN: Hey. You sit about here all day, doing God knows what. I mean, I have no idea. You say you can't read anymore, you can't think, so what? I'm telling you, Terry, I'm tired to death of it, now, it makes up for what we've been losing. All you talk about is leaving, now we can do it. Write back to Victor Frame, and ask him to give you some time, I don't know. Brazil sounds lovely, anything, Terry.

TERRY: Two-fifty? Well, seeing as you got a raise, why don't you get Jackson back? *(beat)*

NAN: What do you mean?

TERRY: Do you know, I spent our last cent getting him sprung? Yes. I let him go, Nan. I sent the man packing.

NAN: I don't understand. Are you trying to tell me you've fired Jackson?

TERRY: Yes, I fired Jackson. Yes!

NAN: Jesus, what the hell is the matter with you? Where the hell do you think the man's going to go? Do you know how long he'll last out there? He has nothing! He has nowhere!

TERRY: *(Vicious, snaps back.)* Yes and we have no money! And Christ, it's enough of this crap, people padding about furtivly, making little plans, this miasma, and I'm so sick of it, I don't care anymore! Waiting for the dusty green Kaffir bus—you should've seen him—I stood here, watching him from this window. Bus after bus, he stood there, couldn't move! Weeping! I mean, finally, I couldn't watch any more. Goodbye Jackson, this stick figure, frozen, terrified, I hate it.

NAN: Oh, Terry, how far do you want to fall? How much...pain do you think you can inflict? I don't think I can take much more.

TERRY: Even with your raise, we're trapped. How much can we save? We owe money all over town! It'll take a year to pay all the bills, and I'm not going to run out on every little shopkeeper in this town. If that's what you expect. Save? We're in the blackhole of Calcutta.

NAN: No. I understand. *(She sits down.)* I've really been so stupid, it's so clear to me now. Here I've been thinking, it'll be okay, once we leave. But the fact of it is, you really don't want to go anywhere, do you? Except a little walk along the beachfront now and then.

TERRY: Pardon?

NAN: Oh, don't. 'Pardon?' Please. I mean, it's all very easy. Jackson's not the frozen and terrified one, really.

TERRY: Let me tell you, I'm being practical, you come in talking about a raise like it's the answer to all our problems, big deal. And that school-mistress tone may work with your home-fucking economics class, but don't ever bring it in here.

NAN: No. Talk to me, don't—

TERRY: *(Shouting, cuts her off.)* Then don't you play at Freud! Don't play at amateur ladies charity tea-shrink-contest-runner up! God, none of your pat little answers and—and the kind of sympathy you reserve for a—

NAN: —how dare you? I mean, all you do is, is take these positions, I mean, talk about clothing yourself in stances, please. At first it's funny, this man rushing out to buy the Beatles, fine, funny, rush out to smoke dope, hipper, always, than all of us. *(beat)* But the thing is, you really love it all. Blenheim, this beachfront, this small world here. It's just this fading of honesty, Terry. I'm sorry. Just stop lying to me! I don't care about you changing your mind, Christ knows I don't want to pack up and move to bloody Brazil. It's the posing. Do you understand? You don't have to do that, we've been married long enough. Just say 'I want to stay.' Because I want you to understand, this whole...wretched...business has been breaking my heart. *(Long pause.)*

TERRY: Not much else to say, eh? It's...you know, the times I—I go for a walk, pass Blenheim, and I'll just stop, remembering what it was like to be a boy there. Holding my cricket kit. In the same spot, fifteen years ago. So happy, so amazed, a boyhood could be so perfect.

I just stand there, here I am, in my thirties, and reduced to memory, already. *(beat)* Well tell me what I should do then? I mean, I don't... I don't know where I belong, is the thing, I thought as kid 'I'm a gentleman farmer, fine' And then, Oh, 'I'm an academic' and I detest the academics—so fine, radical. I'm a radical, right, great.   Make a little radical gesture, hope to join that club, and someone's dead, so— I don't know what to do... I would go back. I would go back and teach. I mean, finally, I only belong at Blenheim, just like Jonathon. I let it...destroy me. Is it so bad? To want to go back? Is it such a... defeat?

NAN: No, of course not. No. It hasn't destroyed you. *(She holds him.)*

TERRY: *(Closes his eyes. Shakes his head.)* I would've...liked to have shown you the Amazon, because you know, it's going. It's the mining. *(beat)* It's... *(Lights fade down. He gasps, reaches for her.)* a whole other world...

FRANKIE AND JOHNNY IN THE CLAIR DE LUNE
by Terrence McNally
Manhattan - Present - Frankie (30's) - Johnny (30's)

Frankie - A woman leary of emotional commitment
Johnny - A man eager for emotional commitment

Frankie and Johnny have shared a night of passion and now
Johnny is making Frankie an egg sandwich. When he burns
himself on the skillet, Frankie is quick to soothe him. Johnny
takes advantage of this situation to work at breaking down
Frankie's emotional barriers.

JOHNNY: Okay. I'll tell you one thing. You didn't miss much not
graduating high school. I had almost two years of college. We both
ended up working for a couple of crazed Greeks. *(He imitates their
boss.)* "Cheeseburger, cheeseburger" is right.
FRANKIE: That was very good.
JOHNNY: Thank you.
FRANKIE: A teacher.
JOHNNY: Hunh?
FRANKIE: What I'm thinking of becoming.
JOHNNY: Why would I laugh at that?
FRANKIE: I don't know. It just seems funny. Someone who can't
spell "cat" teaching little kids to. I'll have to go back to school and
learn before I can teach them but...I don't know, it sounds nice. *(She
hasn't stopped watching Johnny work with the eggs.)* Aren't you going
to scramble them?
JOHNNY: It's better if you just let them set.
FRANKIE: In the restaurant, I've seen you beat 'em. That's when I
noticed you had sexy wrists.
JOHNNY: That's in the restaurant: I'm in a hurry. These are my
special eggs for you. *(He starts cleaning up while the eggs set in a
skillet on the stove top.)*
FRANKIE: You don't have to do that.
JOHNNY: I know.
FRANKIE: Suit yourself.

29

FRANKIE AND JOHNNY IN THE CLAIR DE LUNE

JOHNNY: I bet I know what you're thinking: "He's too good to be true."

FRANKIE: Is that what you want me to think?

JOHNNY: Face it, Frankie, men like me do not grow on trees. Hell, *people* like me don't. *(He holds his wet hands out to her.)* Towel? *(Frankie picks up a dish towel on the counter and begins to dry his hands for him.)* So you think I have sexy wrists?

FRANKIE: I don't think you're gonna break into movies on 'em.

JOHNNY: What do you think is sexy about them?

FRANKIE: I don't know. The shape. The hairs. That vein there. What's that?

JOHNNY: A mole.

FRANKIE: I could live without that.

JOHNNY: First thing Monday morning, it comes off. *(He is kissing her hands. Frankie lets him but keeps a certain distance, too.)*

FRANKIE: Are you keeping some big secret from me?

JOHNNY: It's more like I'm keeping several thousand little ones.

FRANKIE: I'd appreciate a straight answer.

JOHNNY: No, I'm not married.

FRANKIE: Men always think that's the only question women want to ask.

JOHNNY: So fire away.

FRANKIE: Well were you?

JOHNNY: I was.

FRANKIE: How many times?

JOHNNY: Once. Is that it?

FRANKIE: Men have other secrets than being married. You could be a mass murderer or an ex-convict.

JOHNNY: I am. I spent two years in the slammer. Forgery.

FRANKIE: That's okay.

JOHNNY: The state of New Jersey didn't seem to think so.

FRANKIE: It's no skin off my nose.

JOHNNY: Anything else?

FRANKIE: You could be gay.

JOHNNY: Get real, Frankie.

FRANKIE AND JOHNNY IN THE CLAIR DE LUNE

FRANKIE: Well you could!

JOHNNY: Does this look like a gay face?

FRANKIE: You could have a drug problem or a drinking one.

JOHNNY: All right, I did.

FRANKIE: Which one?

JOHNNY: Booze.

FRANKIE: There, you see?

JOHNNY: It's under control now.

FRANKIE: You could still be a real shit underneath all that.

JOHNNY: But I'm not.

FRANKIE: That's your opinion.

JOHNNY: You just want a guarantee we're going to live happily ever after.

FRANKIE: Jesus God knows, I want something. If I was put on this planet to haul hamburgers and french fries to pay the rent on an apartment I don't even like in the vague hope that some stranger will not find me wanting enough not to want to marry me then I think my being born is an experience that is going to be equaled in meaninglessness only by my being dead. I got a whole life ahead of me to feel like this? Excuse me, who do I thank for all this? I think the eggs are ready.

JOHNNY: Everything you said, anybody could say. I could give it back to you in spades. You didn't invent negativity.

FRANKIE: I didn't have to.

JOHNNY: And you didn't discover despair. I was there a long time before you ever heard of it.

FRANKIE: The eggs are burning.

JOHNNY: Fuck the eggs! This is more important!

FRANKIE: I'm hungry! *(Frankie has gone to the stove to take the eggs off. Johnny grabs her from behind and pulls her towards him.)*

JOHNNY: What's the matter with you?

FRANKIE: Let go of me!

JOHNNY: Look at me! *(They struggle briefly. Frankie shoves Johnny who backs into the hot skillet and burns his back.)* Aaaaaaaaaaaaaaa!

FRANKIE: What's the matter—?

31

FRANKIE AND JOHNNY IN THE CLAIR DE LUNE

JOHNNY: Ooooooooooooooo!

FRANKIE: What happened—?

JOHNNY: Ow! Ow! Ow! Ow! Ow! Ow! Ow!

FRANKIE: Oh my God!

JOHNNY: Oooo! Oooo! Oooo! Ooooo! Oooo! Oooooo!

FRANKIE: I'm sorry, I didn't mean to—!

JOHNNY: Jesus, Frankie, Jesus Christ!

FRANKIE: Tell me what to do!

JOHNNY: Get something!

FRANKIE: What?

JOHNNY: Ice.

FRANKIE: Ice for burns? Don't move. *(Frankie puts the entire tray of ice cubes on Johnny's back. The scream that ensues is greater than the first one.)*

JOHNNY: AAAAAAAAAAAAAAAAAAAAAAAAAA!!!!!!!!!!

FRANKIE: You said to—! *(Johnny nods vigorously.)* Should I keep it on? *(Johnny nods again, only this time he bites his fingers to keep from crying out.)* We'd be a terrific couple. One of us would be dead by the end of the first week. One date practically did it. All I asked you to do was turn off the eggs but no! Everything has to be a big deal with you. I would have made the world's worst nurse.

JOHNNY: *(Between gasps of pain.)* Butter.

FRANKIE: What?

JOHNNY: Put some butter on it.

FRANKIE: Butter's bad on burns.

JOHNNY: I don't care.

FRANKIE: I may have some...oh what-do-you-call-it-when-you-have-a-sunburn, it comes in a squat blue bottle?

JOHNNY: Noxzema!

FRANKIE: That's it!

JOHNNY: It breaks me out. Get the butter.

FRANKIE: It's margarine.

JOHNNY: I don't care. *(Frankie gets the margarine out of the refrigerator.)*

FRANKIE: It sounds like you got a lot of allergies.

FRANKIE AND JOHNNY IN THE CLAIR DE LUNE

JOHNNY: Just those three.

FRANKIE: Catsup, Noxzema and...what was the other one?

JOHNNY: Fresh peaches. Canned are okay. *(Frankie puts the margarine on Johnny's back.)* Oooooooooooo!

FRANKIE: Does that feel good?

JOHNNY: You have no idea.

FRANKIE: More?

JOHNNY: Yes, more. Don't stop.

FRANKIE: You're gonna smell like a...whatever a person covered in margarine smells like.

JOHNNY: I don't care.

FRANKIE: To tell the truth, it doesn't look all that bad.

JOHNNY: You think I'm faking this?

FRANKIE: I didn't say that.

JOHNNY: What do you want? Permanent scars? *(Pause. Frankie puts more margarine on Johnny's back.)*

FRANKIE: Did your first wife do this for you?

JOHNNY: Only wife. I told you that.

FRANKIE: Okay, so I was fishing.

JOHNNY: No, checking. Were you married?

FRANKIE: No, never.

JOHNNY: Anyone serious?

FRANKIE: Try "terminal."

JOHNNY: What happened?

FRANKIE: He got more serious with who I thought was my best friend.

JOHNNY: The same thing happened to me.

FRANKIE: You know what the main thing I felt was? Dumb.

JOHNNY: I know, I know!

FRANKIE: I even introduced them. I lent them money. Money from my credit union. I gave her my old television. A perfectly good Zenith. They're probably watching Charles Bronson together at this very moment. I hope it explodes and blows their faces off. No, I don't. I hope it blows up and the fumes kill them. Aren't there suppose to be poison gases in a television set?

33

FRANKIE AND JOHNNY IN THE CLAIR DE LUNE

JOHNNY: I wouldn't be surprised.

FRANKIE: That or he's telling her she looks like shit, who told her she could change her hair or where's his car keys or shut the fuck up, he's had a rough day. I didn't know how exhausting unemployment could be. God, why do we get involved with people it turns out hate us?

JOHNNY: Because...

FRANKIE: ...we hate ourselves. I know. I read the same book.

JOHNNY: How long has it been?

FRANKIE: Seven years. *(Johnny lets out a long stream of air.)* What? You, too? *(Johnny nods.)* Any kids?

JOHNNY: Two.

FRANKIE: You see them?

JOHNNY: Not as much as I'd like. She's remarried. They live in Maine in a beautiful house overlooking the sea.

FRANKIE: I bet it's not so beautiful.

JOHNNY: It's beautiful. I could never have provided them with anything like that. The first time I saw it, I couldn't get out of the car. I felt so ashamed. So forgotten. The kids came running out of the house. They looked so happy to see me but I couldn't feel happy back. All of a sudden, they looked like somebody's else's kids. I couldn't even roll down the window. "What's the matter, daddy?" I started crying. I couldn't stop. Sheila and her husband had to come out of the house to get me to come in. You know what I wanted to do? Run that crewcut asshole insurance salesman over and drive off with the three of them. I don't know where we would've gone. We'd probably still be driving.

FRANKIE: That would've been a dumb thing to do.

JOHNNY: I never said I was smart.

FRANKIE: I'll tell you a secret: you are.

JOHNNY: I said I was passionate. I don't let go of old things easy and I grab new things hard.

FRANKIE: Too hard.

JOHNNY: There's no such thing as too hard when you want something.

34

FRANKIE AND JOHNNY IN THE CLAIR DE LUNE

FRANKIE: Yes, there is, Johnny. The other person. *(There is a pause. Frankie has stopped working on Johnny's back. Instead she just stares at it. Johnny looks straight ahead. The music has changed to the Shostakovich Second String Quartet.)*

JOHNNY: What are you doing back there?

FRANKIE: Nothing. You want more butter or ice or something? *(Johnny shakes his head.)*

JOHNNY: It's funny how you can talk to people better sometimes when you're not looking at them. You're right there. *(He points straight ahead.)* Clear as day.

FRANKIE: I bet no one ever said this was the most beautiful music ever written.

JOHNNY: I don't mind.

FRANKIE: I don't know what the radio was doing on that station in the first place. That's not my kind of music. But I could tell you were enjoying it and I guess I wanted you to think I had higher taste than I really do.

JOHNNY: So did I.

FRANKIE: I liked what he played for us though, but he didn't say its name.

JOHNNY: Maybe it doesn't need one. You just walk into a fancy record shop and ask for the most beautiful music ever written and that's what they hand you.

FRANKIE: Not if I was the salesperson. You'd get "Michelle" or "Eleanor Rigby" or "Lucy In the Sky With Diamonds." Something by the Beatles. I sort of lost interest in pop music when they stopped singing.

JOHNNY: The last record I bought was the Simon and Garfunkel Reunion in Central Park. It wasn't the same. You could tell they'd been separated.

FRANKIE: Sometimes I feel like it's still the Sixties. Or that they were ten or fifteen years ago, not twenty or twenty-five. I lost ten years of my life somewhere. I went to Bruce Springsteen last year and I was the oldest one there.

JOHNNY: Put your arms around me. *(Frankie puts her arms over*

FRANKIE AND JOHNNY IN THE CLAIR DE LUNE

Johnny's shoulders.) Tighter. *(Frankie's hands begin to stroke Johnny's chest and stomach.)* Do you like doing that?

FRANKIE: I don't mind.

JOHNNY: We touch our own bodies there and nothing happens. Something to do with electrons. We short-circuit ourselves. Stroke my tits. There! *(He tilts his head back until he is looking up at her.)* Give me your mouth. *(Frankie bends over and kisses him. It is a long one.)* That tongue. Those lips. *(He pulls her down towards him for another long kiss.)* I want to die like this. Drown.

FRANKIE: What do you want from me?

JOHNNY: Everything. Your heart. Your soul. Your tits. Your mouth. Your fucking guts. I want it all. I want to be inside you. Don't hold back.

FRANKIE: I'm not holding back.

JOHNNY: Let go. I'll catch you.

FRANKIE: I'm right here.

JOHNNY: I want more. I need more.

FRANKIE: If I'd known what playing with your tit was gonna turn into—.

JOHNNY: Quit screwing with me, Frankie.

FRANKIE: You got a pretty weird notion of who's screwing with who. I said I liked you. I told you that. I'm perfectly ready to make love to you. Why do you have to start a big discussion about it. It's not like I am saying "no."

JOHNNY: I want you to do something.

FRANKIE: What?

JOHNNY: I want you to go down on me.

FRANKIE: No.

JOHNNY: I went down on you.

FRANKIE: That was different.

JOHNNY: How?

FRANKIE: That was then.

JOHNNY: Please.

FRANKIE: I'm not good at it.

JOHNNY: Hey, this isn't a contest. We're talking about making love.

FRANKIE AND JOHNNY IN THE CLAIR DE LUNE

FRANKIE: I don't want to right now.

JOHNNY: You want me to go down on you again?

FRANKIE: If I do it will you shut up about all this other stuff?

JOHNNY: You know I won't.

FRANKIE: Then go down on yourself.

JOHNNY: What happened? You were gonna do it.

FRANKIE: Anything to get you to quit picking at me. Go on, get out of here. Get somebody else to go down on you.

JOHNNY: I don't want somebody else to go down on me.

FRANKIE: Jesus! I just had a vision of what it's going to be like at work Monday after this! I'm not quitting my job. I was there first.

JOHNNY: What are you talking about?

FRANKIE: I don't think we're looking for the same thing.

JOHNNY: We are. Only I've found it and you've given up.

FRANKIE: Yes! Long before the sun ever rose on your ugly face.

JOHNNY: What scares you more? Marriage or kids?

FRANKIE: I'm not scared. And I told you: I can't have any.

JOHNNY: I told you: we can adopt.

FRANKIE: I don't love you.

JOHNNY: That wasn't the question.

FRANKIE: You hear what *you* want to hear.

JOHNNY: Do you know anybody who doesn't?

FRANKIE: Not all the time.

JOHNNY: You're only telling me you don't love me so you don't have to find out if you could. Just because you've given up on the possibility, I'm not going to let you drag me down with you. You're coming up to my level if I have to pull you by the hair.

FRANKIE: I'm not going anywhere with a man who for all his bullshit about marriage and kids and Shakespeare...

JOHNNY: It's not bullshit!

FRANKIE: ...Just wants me to go down on him.

JOHNNY: Pretend it was a metaphor.

FRANKIE: Fuck you it was a metaphor! It was a blowjob. What's a metaphor?

JOHNNY: Something that stands for something else.

37

FRANKIE AND JOHNNY IN THE CLAIR DE LUNE

FRANKIE: I was right the first time. A blowjob.

JOHNNY: A sensual metaphor for mutual acceptance.

FRANKIE: Fuck you. Besides, what's mutual about a blowjob?

JOHNNY: I made that up. I'm sorry. It wasn't a metaphor. It was just something I wanted us to do.

FRANKIE: And I didn't.

JOHNNY: Let go, will you! One lousy little peccadillo and it's off with his head!

FRANKIE: Stop using words I don't know. What's a peccadillo?

JOHNNY: A blowjob! Notice I haven't died you didn't do it!

FRANKIE: I noticed.

JOHNNY: And let me notice something for you: you wouldn't have died if you had. Thanks for making me feel about this big. *(He gets up and starts gathering and putting on his clothes.)* I'm sorry, I mistook you for a kindred spirit. Kindred: two of a kind, sharing a great affinity.

FRANKIE: I know what kindred means!

JOHNNY: Shall we go for affinity!

FRANKIE: That's the first really rotten thing you've said all night. Somebody who would make fun of somebody else's intelligence, no worse, their education or lack of—that is somebody I would be very glad not to know. I thought you were weird, Johnny. I thought you were sad. I didn't think you were cruel.

JOHNNY: I'm sorry.

FRANKIE: It's a cruelty just waiting to happen again and I don't want to be there when it does.

JOHNNY: Please! *(There is an urgency in his voice that startles Frankie.)* I'm not good with people. But I want to be. I can get away with it for long stretches but I always hang myself in the end.

FRANKIE: Hey, c'm'on, don't cry. Please, don't cry.

JOHNNY: It's not cruelty. It's a feeling I don't matter. That nobody hears me. I'm drowning. I'm trying to swim back to shore but there's this tremendous undertow and I'm not getting anywhere. My arms and legs are going a mile a minute but they aren't taking me any closer to where I want to be.

38

FRANKIE AND JOHNNY IN THE CLAIR DE LUNE

FRANKIE: Where's that?

JOHNNY: With you.

FRANKIE: You don't know me.

JOHNNY: Yes, I do. It scares people how much we really know one another, so we pretend we don't. You know me. You've known me all your life. Only now I'm here. Take me. Use me. Try me. There's a reason we're called Frankie and Johnny.

FRANKIE: There's a million other Frankies out there and a billion other Johnnys. The world is filled with Frankies and Johnnys and Jacks and Jills.

JOHNNY: But only one this Johnny, one this Frankie.

FRANKIE: We're too different.

JOHNNY: You say po-tah-toes? All right, I'll say po-tah-toes! I don't care. I love you. I want to marry you.

FRANKIE: I don't say po-tah-toes. Who the hell says po-tah-toes?

JOHNNY: Are you listening to me?

FRANKIE: I'm trying very hard not to!

JOHNNY: That's your trouble. You don't want to hear anything you don't think you already know. Well I'll tell you something, Cinderella: Your Prince Charming has come. Wake up before another thousand years go by! Don't throw me away like a gum wrapper because you think there's something about me you may not like. I have what it takes to give you anything and everything you want. Maybe not up here... *(He taps his head.)* ...or here... *(He slaps his hip where he wears his wallet.)* ...but here. And that would please me enormously. All I ask back is that you use your capacity to be everyone and everything for me. It's within you. If we could do that for each other we'd give our kids the universe. They'd be Shakespeare and the most beautiful music ever written and a saint maybe or a champion athlete or a president all rolled into one. Terrific kids! How could they not be? We have a chance to make everything turn out all right again. Turn our backs on everything that went wrong. We can begin right now and all over again but only if we begin right now, this minute, this room and us. I know this thing, Frankie.

FRANKIE: I want to show you something, Johnny. *(She pushes her hair back.)* He did that. The man I told you about. With a belt buckle. *(Johnny kisses the scar.)*

JOHNNY: It's gone now.

FRANKIE: It'll never go.

JOHNNY: It's gone. I made it go.

FRANKIE: What are you? My guardian angel?

JOHNNY: It seems to me the right people are our guardian angels.

FRANKIE: I wanted things, too, you know.

JOHNNY: I know.

FRANKIE: A man, a family, kids... He's the reason I can't have any.

JOHNNY: He's gone. Choose me. Hurry up. It's getting light out. I turn into a pumpkin.

FRANKIE: *(Looking towards the window.)* It is getting light out! *(Frankie goes to the window.)*

JOHNNY: You are so beautiful standing there.

FRANKIE: The only time I saw the sun come up with a guy was my senior prom. *(Johnny has joined her at the window. As they stand there looking out, we will be aware of the rising sun.)* His name was Johnny Di Corso but everyone called him Skunk. *(She takes Johnny's hand and clasps it to her but her eyes stay looking out the window at the dawn.)* He was a head shorter than me and wasn't much to look at but nobody else had asked me. It was him or else. I was dreading it. But guess what? That boy could dance! You should have seen us. We were the stars of the prom. We did Lindys, the Mambo, the Twist. The Monkey, the Frug. All the fast dances. Everybody's mouth was down to here. Afterwards we went out to the lake to watch the sun come up. He told me he was going to be on American Bandstand one day. I wonder if he ever made it. *(Johnny puts his arm around her and begins to move her in a slow dance step.)*

JOHNNY: There must be something about you and sunrises and men called Johnny.

FRANKIE: You got a nickname?

JOHNNY: No. You got to be really popular or really unpopular to have a nickname.

FRANKIE: I'll give you a nickname. *(They dance in silence a while.*

40

Silence, that is, except for the Shostakovich which they pay no attention to.) You're not going to like me saying this but you're a terrible dancer.

JOHNNY: Show me.

FRANKIE: Like that.

JOHNNY: There?

FRANKIE: That's better.

JOHNNY: You're going to make a wonderful teacher. *(He starts to hum.)*

HENCEFORWARD...
by Alan Ayckbourn
Jerome's "computerized fortress" - Future - Jerome (40) - Zoe (30's)

Jerome - An eccentric composer and electronics wizard
Zöe - An actress

Jerome has an artistic block because his wife left him and took
his inspiration, their daughter. To get visitation rights, he hires
an actress to play his wife and present the picture of domestic
bliss to the Child Welfare Department. Here, Zoë, the actress
hired to play Jerome's wife, decides to get to know Jerome
better, maybe even intimately.

JEROME: Here.
ZOË: *(Recoiling)* Ah!
JEROME: You OK?
ZOË: Yes—it was—hot.
JEROME: Good. I brought some beer. I thought you'd prefer the can
rather than our glasses. *(He opens both the meals.)* That's yours. I
think.
ZOË: Thank you.
JEROME: *(Examining his own dish)* Yes, I think these must be the
wild strawberries. Do you want beer?
ZOË: Please.
(JEROME opens the beers.)
JEROME: Go ahead, do start. Before it gets rusty.
(She tries it.)
ZOË: Mmm! Not bad.
JEROME: Hot enough?
ZOË: Perfect. *(They eat.)* How long were you married? To Corinna?
JEROME: Eleven years.
ZOË: God. A lifetime. Must have felt very strange. Splitting up.
JEROME: Yes.
ZOË: I mean, even if you loathed the sight of each other.
JEROME: Yes.
ZOË: Was she a musician?

42

HENCEFORWARD...

JEROME: Corinna? *(He laughs.)* No. She was my bank manager. Until I moved my account.

ZOË: Do you miss her?

JEROME: No.

ZOË: Would you ever consider going back to her?

JEROME: Look, what the hell is this? A census?

ZOË: I just want to know. I need to know.

JEROME: Why? Why do you want to know all that?

ZOË: Because I'll need to. If I'm to behave like someone who's been living with you for some time, I'll need to know.

JEROME: Well, you don't need to know all that. I'll tell you what you need to know, don't worry.

ZOË: OK. Fine. Fire ahead.

(A pause.)

JEROME: *(Grumpily)* What do you want to know?

ZOË: No, no. I'm not asking any more questions. You tell me.

JEROME: It's all right...

ZOË: No, if I ask questions you just bite my head off. You can tell me, go on.

JEROME: I'm sorry. I—I haven't really talked to anyone—well, not face to face—for some time, you see. Since they fully automated the hypermarket, I don't think I've spoken to anyone for months. So, you'll have to make allowances.

ZOË: I understand.

JEROME: So. If you want to ask questions. Please.

ZOË: Right.

(They eat)

JEROME: Go ahead.

ZOË: I will. I'm just trying to think of some. Why did your wife leave you?

JEROME: I don't think that's any of your damn business.

ZOË: Oh, terrific... Forget it. I'll just make it up. I'll make it all up. Just don't blame me if it all goes totally wrong. When it turns out that I don't know vital facts about you that I should know—

JEROME: I just don't see that you need to—

43

HENCEFORWARD...

ZOË: Look. If it transpires that your wife left you because for eleven years—or whatever it was—you drove her absolutely mad whistling in the nude at breakfast time—then that's something I ought to know. Because it just might crop up in converstaion between the two of us. 'Darling, doesn't he drive you mad the way he whistles in the nude at breakfast?' 'No, not at all, dear, I love it, I find it totally refreshing...'

JEROME: All right, all right. My wife left me because... She claimed I drove her mad—

ZOË: Whistling in the nude at breakfast—? Sorry.

JEROME: She wasn't, in the end, prepared to live with a creative person. That's what it boiled down to. She wasn't prepared to fit in with the lifestyle of a creative entity. Such as myself. That's all. I'm not saying she was a selfish woman. Nor am I saying she was a woman who refused to adapt or even begin to understand the pressures that—a creative person can undergo. I'm not saying that about her. After all, why should she? She's just a bloody bank manager.

ZOË: *(Sympathetically)* No. And you probably didn't understand a lot about banking, did you?

JEROME: *(Sharply)* What's that got to do with it?

ZOË: *(Quickly)* Nothing.

JEROME: Still, I'm sure she'll make some—chief clerk—a very good wife.

ZOË: *(Deciding this isn't a line worth pursuing further)* I'd love to hear some of your music. Could I, possibly?

JEROME: Yes. Perhaps. Sometime. As I say, I haven't written anything for—ages.

ZOË: Since they left?

JEROME: Nearly.

ZOË: Four years. Heavens. You really did need them, then, in some ways? Well, your muse did.

JEROME: Geain. I needed Geain. I need her back more than anything in the world.

(ZOË, for the first time, notices the signs of his inner distress.)

ZOË: *(Moved)* Well, I'll—do my best for you. *(Pause.)* Did she inspire your Singing Babies? I bet she did.

HENCEFORWARD...

JEROME: *First Sounds.* Yes. *(Pause.)* I recorded her over several days...

ZOË: You mean it was actually her? Actually Geain you used?

JEROME: Yes. That was the first occasion I started using purely natural sounds—sampling and treating them. It took months.

ZOË: Fancy. And all that for what? Thirty seconds?

JEROME: Thirty seconds? It was a forty-five minute piece originally.

ZOË: Oh, I see. There's more?

JEROME: Much, much, much more.

ZOË: You can't write at all, then? No ideas?

JEROME: I know what I want to write. But I don't know how to do it.

ZOË: What?

JEROME: *(More to himself)* I know what it's going to be. I know what I want to say. It's how to say it. I haven't got the sound. I haven't heard it. Three years and I'm still waiting to hear the sound.

ZOË: What do you want to say?

JEROME: I want to say—what I want to say is—well, I want to say—love. Really.

ZOË: *(Mystified)* Love?

JEROME: Yes.

ZOË: I see. What sort of love?

JEROME: Just—generally. Love. You know...

ZOË: *(Puzzled)* No, I'm not sure I—

JEROME: *(Tetchily)* Love. You've heard of love, I presume?

ZOË: Yes, yes. Sorry, only you're not putting it awfully well.

JEROME: *(Irritably)* Of course I'm not putting it awfully well. If I could put it awfully well, there wouldn't be a problem. I want to express the feeling of love in an abstract musical form. In such a way that anyone who hears it—*anyone*—no matter what language they speak—no matter what creed or colour—they will recognize it—and respond to it—and relate it to their own feelings of love that they have or they've experienced at some time—so they say—yes, my God, that's it! That's what it is! And maybe who knows, consequently, there might be a bit more of it.

45

HENCEFORWARD...

(ZOË is spellbound by this.)

ZOË: How wonderful. *(She reflects for a second.)* It must have been a bit like this, sitting with Beethoven.

JEROME: I doubt it.

ZOË: That's how I imagine it, anyway.

JEROME: I don't think Beethoven sat down all that much. He used to stamp about the place, shouting.

ZOË: There you are, then. You're both terribly similar. *(Pause. They have both finished their meal.)* Oh, it must be just so awful for you. Having all those ideas and not being able to express them. Poor you. *(JEROME looks at her.)* I mean, I know sort of how you feel. I get that way if I'm just writing a letter. I want to say something really—I don't know—heartfelt to someone. And it all comes out like the inside of some awful Christmas card. Happy tidings, boyfriend dear. At this joyous time of year. When what you mean to say is—I love you incredibly much and I'd do just about everything I could in the world to make you happy and I just want to be with you and stay close to you for ever and ever and ever— And you try and write that down so it makes sense and what do you get? Happy tidings, boyfriend dear... *(Aware of his gaze)* What's the matter?

JEROME: Nothing.

ZOË: Are you having second thoughts?

JEROME: No. Third thoughts.

ZOË: *(Slightly apprehensive)* Oh? What are those?

JEROME: I was just thinking—you're a very nice person, really. Only, saying it like that, I think I sound rather like one of your Christmas cards.

(A pause. ZOË is a little ill at ease.)

ZOË: I think I'll sing my song for you now, if you don't mind.

JEROME: *(Rather dismayed)* Really?

ZOË: Well, it's either that or my Shakespeare. And I don't think Queen Margaret would go down frightfully well after chicken and strawberries. *(Arranging herself)* It's all right, it's quite short... *(Making a false start)* You're not my—Hang on. *(She sorts out her first note.)* Right. Here we go. *(Sings:)*

HENCEFORWARD...

You're not my first love...
It would only be a lie if I pretended—
In the past there have been others
Who have slept between these covers
But I promise
Though you're far too late in life to be my first love,
You'll be my last love.
I swear to you, you're gonna be my last love...

(She finishes her song. Silence.) Well. It has this great accompaniment. Diddly-diddly diddly dom. *(She smiles at him awkwardly. JEROME rises and moves to her. He stands by her, then kisses her. They break and stare at each other.)* You taste of wild strawberries.

JEROME: You tast of grouse. *(ZOË Laughs. JEROME smiles one of his rare smiles.)* Do you want any more?

ZOË: More?

JEROME: Food?

ZOË: No.

JEROME: Any more anything of anything?

ZOË: *(Without hesitation)* Yes, please.

JEROME: Well, shall we...? What would you prefer to do? I mean, would you like to—here? Or—?

ZOË: I don't mind. Here's fine if—you—

JEROME: Or there's the bedroom, that might be—

ZOË: Sure. That's fine. Will she have made the bed by now, do you think? *(She laughs.)*

JEROME: Oh, no, that's no problem. Those sheets were just for her to—

ZOË: Well, fine. Shall we in there?

JEROME: *(Unmoving)* Yes, yes, yes.

ZOË: You want to?

JEROME: Oh, yes. You bet.

ZOË: I mean, we don't have to if you—?

JEROME: No, no, no... *(Laughing)* Useful research, whatever else...

ZOË: *(Drawing back, concerned)* Oh, I wasn't...just for that.

JEROME: No, no. I was joking.
ZOË: I mean, I really want to. I don't—if I don't want to...I don't do that sort of thing.
JEROME: I know, I'm sure. Nor do I.
ZOË: Good. *(Pause.)* Well—shall we...?
JEROME: Why not?

HURLYBURLY
by David Rabe
Los Angeles - Present - Eddie (30's) - Darlene (30's)

Eddie - A casting agent
Darlene - Eddie's girlfriend

Darlene has confessed to having been raped many years ago to
Eddie, who seems to have taken the news well until an argument
about where to eat seems to indicate otherwise.

DARLENE: *(standing up, she bolts for the kitchen)* I'm hungry. You
hungry?
EDDIE: I mean, if we don't talk these things out, we'll just end up
with all this, you know, unspoken shit, following us around. *(following
her)* You wanna go out and eat? Let's go out. What are you hungry
for? How about Chinese?
DARLENE: Sure. *(In the kitchen, she is rummaging for something to
nibble on.)*
EDDIE: *(heading back to the phone on which is on the coffee table)*
We could go to Mr. Chou's. Treat ourselves right.
DARLENE: That's great. I love the seaweed. *(digging open a bag
of pretzels)*
EDDIE: I mean, you want Chinese?
DARLENE: I love Mr. Chou's.
EDDIE: We could go some other place. How about Ma Maison?
DARLENE: Sure.
EDDIE: *(running to the rolodex on the counter)* You like that better
than Mr. Chou's?
DARLENE: *(increasingly irritated)* It doen't matter to me.
EDDIE: Which one should I call?
DARLENE: Surprise me.
EDDIE: I don't want to surprise you. I want to, you know, do
whatever you really want.
DARLENE: Then just pick one. Call one. Either.
EDDIE: I mean, why should I have to guess? I don't want to guess.
Just tell me. I mean, what if I pick the wrong one? *(heading back to*

49

the coffee table and phone)
DARLENE: You can't pick the wrong one. Honestly, Eddie, I like them both the same. I like them both exactly the same.
EDDIE: *(freezing)* Exactly?
DARLENE: Yes. I like them both.
EDDIE: I mean, how can you possibly think you like them both the same? One is French and one is Chinese. They're different. They're as different as— *(crossing back to her)* I mean, what is the world, one big blur to you out there in which everything that bears some resemblance to something else is just automatically put at the same level in your hierarchy, for chrissake, Darlene, the only thing they have in common is that THEY'RE BOTH RESTAURANTS!
DARLENE: Are you aware that you're yelling?
EDDIE: *(crossing back to the phone)* My voice is raised for emphasis, which is a perfectly legitimate use of volume. Particularly when, in addition, I evidently have to break through this goddamn cloud in which you are obviously enveloped in which everything is just this blur totally devoid of the most rudimentary sort of distinction. *(He is rooting through the rolodex as she rushes over.)*
DARLENE: *(Grabbing the phone, she sticks it into his hand.)* Just call the restaurant, why don't you?
EDDIE: Why are you doing this?
DARLENE: I'm hungry. I'm just trying to get something to eat before I faint.
EDDIE: The fuck you are. You're up to something.
DARLENE: What do you mean, what am I up to? You're telling me I don't know if I'm hungry or not? I'm hungry.!
EDDIE: Bullshit!
DARLENE: "Up to?" Paranoia, Eddie. Para-fuckin-noia. Be alert. Your tendencies are coming out all over the place.
EDDIE: I'm fine.
DARLENE: I mean, to stand there screeching at me about what-am-I-up-to is paranoid.
EDDIE: Not, if you're up to something, it's not.
DARLENE: *(storming away toward the counter, the pretzels, the wine)*

I'm not. Take my word for it, you're acting a little nuts.

EDDIE: Oh, I'm supposed to trust your judgment of my mental stability? *(He is advancing on her as she pours her wine.)* I'm supposed to trust your evaluation of the nuances of my sanity? You can't even tell the difference between a French and a Chinese restaurant!

DARLENE: I like them both. *(With her wine and pretzels she heads for the couch, flopping down on the S.L. end.)*

EDDIE: But they're different! One is French, and the other is Chinese. THEY'RE TOTALLY FUCKING DIFFERENT!

DARLENE: NOT IN MY INNER EMOTIONAL SUBJECTIVE EXPERIENCE OF THEM!

EDDIE: *(He moves behind the couch, talking into the back of her head, then around to face her from the S.R. side.)* The tastes, the decors, the waiters, the accents. The fucking accents. The little phrases the waiters say. And they yell at each other in these whole totally different languages, does none of this make an impression on you?!

DARLENE: It impresses me that I like them both.

EDDIE: Your total inner emotional subjective experience must be THIS EPIC FUCKING FOG! I mean, what are you on, some sort of dualistic trip and everything is in two's and you just can't tell which is which so you're just pulled taut between them on this goddamn high wire between people who might like to have some kind of definitive reaction from you in order to know!

DARLENE: Fuck you!

IS HE STILL DEAD?
by Donald Freed
A hotel in France - 1940 - James Joyce (58) - Nora Joyce (50's)

James Joyce - An author
Nora Joyce - James Joyce's wife

Two months before his death, James Joyce and his wife, Nora, discuss the plight of their daughter, Lucia, who has been commited to a mental clinic. Distressed at their lack of funds, they worry about the future.

JOYCE: There's no money to pay her clinic bill, leave alone getting her transferred to French Switzerland, and we don't even—
NORA: Jaysus, will you dry up for once and use your "world-famous" brain to put two and two to—
JOYCE: —And they want to call her mad because she believes she's being left to—
NORA: —Try not to go off your own head—
JOYCE: —Monsters coming to destroy her, and it's true! There are, they're—
NORA: —Have you gone mad yourself?
JOYCE: —How can I leave her there— What if they put her out before we can send for her— My God, it's tearing me in half—
NORA: You? Can't you think of someone, for once, besides yourself?!
JOYCE: The Germans—the Germans are coming, you foolish woman—
NORA: Your daughter!— Can't you think of your daughter—and what's best for her?
JOYCE: You hate her because she's an artist—like me. Let's have the truth at last!
(JOYCE is doubled over, gasping from the ordeal. NORA stalks in and out of the bedroom, dressing to go out, muttering to herself in wild agitation.)
NORA: *(Stunned, then walking)* That's the last straw. The Pernod's rotted his brain. He's gone too far, now. He's burned his bridges, now. I hate you—that's the holy truth of it: with yer "clinic," and yer

IS HE STILL DEAD?

"maison de sante," and yer "maison de repos"—in the name of Christ, man, when will ye face it and use the hard word: Our daughter is not an "artist" she's a poor lunatic in a lunatic asylum!

JOYCE: Help!

NORA: Didn't she try to murder me—

JOYCE: Don't you blame me—

NORA: My own child—

JOYCE: I visited her—you never did!

NORA: Picked up the chair—

(He pounds out a tune on the piano.)

NORA: —with the strength of ten— *(Picking up a chair, slowly, as if in a nightmare)* Picked up the chair and threw it-at-my-head!

(NORA's strangled cry cuts through the piano sound. Then, a long silence, and she turns to leave. JOYCE stumbles about, pushing over luggage.)

JOYCE: *(Continuing; gasping after her.)* That's it—leave us.

NORA: *(Walking and cursing)* "...hour of our death, Amen," he's mad and he's driven her mad, and he's trying to drive me mad—

JOYCE: Where are you sneaking away to, now?

NORA: *(Stopping)* I am walking to Mass.

JOYCE: Crawling, you mean.

NORA: Rave on, but it's her religion she needs now.

JOYCE: Who?

NORA: Our daughter, who d'ye think?

JOYCE: Which religion? There're a hundred and forty-two known religions. And what good would it do her?

NORA: Give her a bit of hope, which is more than you've done. And help her to face the next life.

JOYCE: WHAT ABOUT THIS LIFE?! —And how could I give her any hope when I've none myself?

NORA: You've never known your own daughter.

JOYCE: Allow me to say, I was present at her conception.

NORA: You know nothin' at all about women.

JOYCE: I know all that can be known.

NORA: And I know the rest! —Sure, you've not a clue about your

53

own self, so how could you understand anything about Lucia?
JOYCE: Lucia does not need "understanding"—Lucia needs love!
NORA: Words! I'm—away—now—to—
JOYCE: Mass, I know. Dominick go frisk him! My God, the woman still believes in banshees and the Holy Ghost!
NORA: Shut yer gob.
JOYCE: To pray for her?
(First NORA, then JOYCE, breaks down.)
NORA: To pray for all of us.
(JOYCE collapses in her arms.)
JOYCE: The book, the book, I traded my daughter's youth for that book!
NORA: *(She rocks him like a child.)* Wisha, Jim, hush, hush...
JOYCE: Never a real home—no country, no language, no friends—
NORA: We've made our bed, Jim...
JOYCE: The drink!—I traded her soul to the devil. The virginity of her soul! —For the book! The critics were right—I'm not a writer at all, I'm a devil!
NORA: Yes, you're a "Great Sinner"—except you're not—you're just an ordinary one. *(A bitter laugh)*
JOYCE: You're a cruel woman! Trot away now to Mass, and chat up the priest.
NORA: You're pathetic. *(She starts to leave.)*
JOYCE: "Pray in your closet."
NORA: Raving.
JOYCE: The Bible says—"Pray in your—"
NORA: You pray in your closet!
JOYCE: I would if I had one.
NORA: A closet?
JOYCE: No. A soul.
NORA: You poor fellah, you—no one has a soul, until they've confessed their sins, and Communion taken.
JOYCE: What? What is there left for me to confess?
NORA: *(Coming back to him, she speaks softly to his heart or soul.)* Yourself.

IS HE STILL DEAD?

JOYCE: Myself?

NORA: I'm not talkin' about the guilt—the drink and the writing and the guilt. I'm referrin' to Jimmy Joyce—the man.

(He shakes, then kneels in front of her like a child.)

NORA: *(Continuing)* Jim, get up now!

JOYCE: I confess.

NORA: Have you no shame, at all?

(His tone stuns her. He is not mocking.)

JOYCE: No!—I confess... You hear my confession. You give me my forgiveness. Not a priest—you!

NORA: Jim, what are you doing? —I can't forgive you. I can't give—

JOYCE: Only you—

NORA: —can't give you Communion. I'm only—

JOYCE: I'll take anything! *(A sobbing laugh; he clings to her dress.)*

NORA: Let me go, now—

JOYCE: No! I confess!

NORA: Then go and do it!

(She rips away from him. He falls over on all fours, crawls a few feet, then, like a beast in pain, he tries to pray. He makes only strange sounds.)

NORA: *(Continuing)* Christ have pity on the poor thing...

JOYCE: *(His voice is strangled.)* Christ have mercy...

(NORA sways with the shared pain. She fights to keep her voice private and under control. His words are like a death rattle.)

NORA: "Holy Mary, pray for him..."

JOYCE: "All you holy Angels and Archangels, pray for..."

NORA: "St. Joseph..." Oh, please, don't let him die, now...

JOYCE: "St. Mary Magdalene..."

NORA: —let him die in Zurich—where we began...

JOYCE: "Through your death and burial... Run out to meet her, Angels of the Lord..."

(He vomits dryly, in spasms of grief.)

NORA: —let them both die there...

(Slowly, like an animal, his panting subsides. Then, he looks up with

55

IS HE STILL DEAD?

exhausted cunning.)
JOYCE: Will you give me the Communion, now?
(NORA is wary. She brings a towel to wipe his face. He looks up at her.)
NORA: What is it you're after, now?... What d'ye want from me, Jim?
JOYCE: Everything: Open my tomb—speak in tongues—fill me with the Holy Ghost—erection and resurrection—ravish my soul—put your wafer in my mouth...
(NORA stares down at the mad outburst with a cold control.)
NORA: What else?
JOYCE: Sing a dirty song for me.
NORA: *(Pause, a whisper)* Oh, you're as cute as a shit-house rat!— You want me to beat you—but I won't.
(He laughs silently, shaking his head, then lets her help him up. She has to guide him to the sofa.)
NORA: No... No, I'm a dead man. Dead and rotten...
NORA: Wisha, Jim, give over. —You're not a great sinner, you're a great writer, that's all, the greatest writer in the world. It's not your fault. It's no one's fault, and that's the short of it.
JOYCE: Just let me die—and sell the manuscripts.
NORA: Sure, you're worth more dead that alive. *(A sad laugh)* We all are. That's the truth: We're all dying. —But I wouldn't give the critics the satisfaction.

KEY EXCHANGE
by Kevin Wade
Central Park, NYC - Present - Philip (30's) - Lisa (30's)

Philip - A man trying to make up with his lover
Lisa - Philip's lover

Lisa and Philip have a relationship that she would very much like to make permanent. They have recently quarreled about their situation and the future. Here, Philip attempts to reconcile with Lisa.

PHILIP: Lisa! LISA! *(A moment, as he decides whether to wait and see if she stops or get his bicycle and give chase)* LISA! Please don't pass! *(Philip tears back up-stage and rights his bicycle. Lisa enters, stage right. Philip turns to go, sees her, stops)*
LISA: I cut back around. Hi. How are you?
PHILIP: Good. You?
LISA: Fine.
PHILIP: I tried to call you all last week. Stopped by a couple of times. Well, more than a couple.
LISA: I was out of town.
PHILIP: I figured that. Work?
LISA: A friend is doing a piece on the Newport regatta. I photographed it for him.
PHILIP: Terrific.
LISA: It was pretty boring, mostly. We spent one day on the water, following the boats, which was great. Spent five days in Newpy, as they call it, talking to all these Republicans with three or four names and those alligator shirts. It was nice to get out, though. *(Pause)* How's the novel coming?
PHILIP: It's finished.
LISA: Really?
PHILIP: Yeah, it's all done.
LISA: That's wonderful. That's so exciting! *(Lays down her bicycle)* How does it come out? No, don't tell me, I want to read it. Can I read it?

KEY EXCHANGE

PHILIP: *(Laying down his bicycle)* I wish you would.

LISA: What's it called?

PHILIP: Either "Shotgun Wedding" or "The Bride Came D.O.A."

LISA: *(After a moment)* They're both good.

(Pause)

PHILIP: I'm sorry about that phone call last week, waking you up.

LISA: That's okay.

PHILIP: I'm sorry about a lot of things.

LISA: Listen you, cut that out. Do I have to read you the No Regrets Clause?

PHILIP: *(Laughs, a little)* No.

LISA: I mean, you wrote the damn thing.

PHILIP: Right. I want to be with you.

LISA: We tried that. It didn't work.

PHILIP: I didn't really try, though. I can do much better.

LISA: It's not a question of better or worse.

PHILIP: I mean, if you give me half a chance, I could really make a go of it and not just...

LISA: Oh, Philip, wait a minute. *(Goes to him)* Sit with me. *(They sit. She kisses him, lightly)* Hello.

PHILIP: Hello.

LISA: *(Kisses him again, on the forehead)* That night I asked you to come to dinner with my father, and you went into that whole theory about, what did you say, some primal instinct to protect the brood...

PHILIP: I got a little carried away there. I wish I...

LISA: Hold it. I went to meet him alone, and after I sat down the first thing he said was , "So where's this Philip character? What is it, he's sleeping with my daughter and he's too chicken to come and meet her maker?"

PHILIP: Oh.

LISA: Aren't you going to say I told you so?

PHILIP: No. *(Pause)* I love you.

LISA: *(Squeezing his hand)* And I love you too, you nut, you and your amateur anthropology.

PHILIP: No, I mean it, I love you and I want to...

KEY EXCHANGE

LISA: *(Puts a finger to his lips, shifts around and kneels, taking his hands)* I mean it too. You're a wonderful man, and very dear in your way, and that's the way I want to see you. I want to enjoy the Philip that I met, and not try to mold him into The Right Man for Me. *(Pause)* I can't be with you as a couple. It was so much effort, and I finally realized that we're two folks who care about each other very much but who, well, it's like we can rock and roll all over the floor just fine but we can't quite find a way to dance close and in time without stepping on each other's feet. You know what I mean? *(Pause)* I want to think that I can see you and ride with you and be close. And I really want to read "The Bride Came D.O.A."

PHILIP: You think that's it?

LISA: Definitely. *(Kisses him)* I have to go.

PHILIP: I, Jesus, this is all a little fast. Can I see you tonight?

LISA: I have to be in the darkroom all night. I have a mile of film to develop and prints to make.

PHILIP: I won't get in your way. I need to talk to you some more.

LISA: John, he's the guy who's writing the piece, he has to be there to look at the contacts. It has to be ready for tomorrow noon.

PHILIP: How about after? I'll buy you a drink.

LISA: It'll go late.

PHILIP: Ring me when you're almost done, I'll start on over.

LISA: Philip. It'll go overnight.

PHILIP: Oh, I see.

LISA: *(She hugs him, speaking over his shoulder)* It has nothing to do with what I just said. Nothing at all. Okay? Do you know that?

PHILIP: Sure, you say so.

LISA: I'll call you next week. Maybe we could take a tour out to the country, take in some nature.

PHILIP: Okay. Maybe. I...damn.

LISA: We'll talk. We'll see. *(Kisses him, hugs him hard)* Bye.

(She gets up, crosses quickly to her bicycle, hurries it down to the road, pauses, waves without turning around, exits. Philip moves to his left, watches her go)

LES LIAISONS DANGEREUSES
by Christopher Hampton
Paris - 1780's - Valmont (30's) - Tourvel (22)

Valmont - A rascal
Tourvel - An elegant lady

Valmont and his cohort, Merteuil, play games of sexual intrigue
and conquest, until Valmont is finally destroyed by love. Here,
Valmont makes his first move on the pristine Tourvel.

TOURVEL: I can't understand how someone whose instincts are so
generous could lead such a dissolute life.

VALMONT: I'm afraid you have an exaggerated idea both of my
generosity and of my depravity. If I knew who'd given you such a dire
account of me, I might be able to defend myself; since I don't, let me
make a confession: I'm afraid the key to the paradox lies in a certain
weakness of character.

TOURVEL: I don't see how so thoughtful an act of charity could be
described as weak.

VALMONT: This appalling reputation of mine, you see, there is some
justification for it. I've spent my life surrounded by immoral people;
I've allowed myself to be influenced by them and sometimes even taken
pride in outshining them. Whereas, in this case, I've simply fallen
under a quite opposite kind of influence: yours.

TOURVEL: You mean you wouldn't have done it...?

VALMONT: Not without your example, no. It was by way of an
innocent tribute to your goodness. *(There's a pause, during which
MME DE TOURVEL, uncertain how to react, abandons her tapestry,
hovers indecisively for a second and then sits, perching on the edge of
a chaise-longue.)* You see how weak I am? I promised myself I was
never going to tell you. It's just, looking at you...

TOURVEL: Monsieur.

VALMONT: You needn't worry, I have no illicit intentions, I wouldn't
dream of insulting you. But I do love you. I adore you. *(He's across
the room in an instant, drops to one knee in front of her and takes her
hands in his.)* Please help me! *(MME DE TOURVEL wrenches her*

hands free and bursts into tears.) What is it?

TOURVEL: I'm so unhappy! *(She buries her face in her hands, sobbing. For an instant, a shadow of a smile twitches across VALMONT's face, before he speaks in a voice on the edge of tears.)*

VALMONT: But why?

TOURVEL: Will you leave me now? *(VALMONT rises and moves away across the room, ostensibly making an effort to control himself.)*

VALMONT: I shouldn't have said anything, I know I shouldn't, I'm sorry. But really, you have nothing to fear. Nothing at all. Tell me what to do, show me how to behave, I'll do anything you say. *(MME DE TOURVEL manages to control herself and looks up at him.)*

TOURVEL: I thought the least I could hope for was that you would respect me.

VALMONT: But I do, of course I do!

TOURVEL: Then forget all this, don't say another word, you've offended me deeply, it's unforgivable.

VALMONT: I thought you might at least give me some credit for being honest.

TOURVEL: On the contrary, this confirms everything I've been told about you. I'm beginning to think you may well have planned the whole exercise.

VALMONT: When I came to visit my aunt, I had no idea you were here: not that it would have disturbed me in the slightest if I had known. You see, up until then, I'd only ever experienced desire. Love, never.

TOURVEL: That's enough.

VALMONT: No, no, you made an accusation, you must allow me the opportunity to defend myself. Now, you were there when my aunt asked me to stay a little longer, and at that time I only agreed in deference to her, although I was already by no means unaware of your beauty.

TOURVEL: Monsieur...

VALMONT: No, the point is, all this has nothing to do with your beauty. As I got to know you, I began to realize that beauty is the least of your qualities. I became fascinated by your goodness, I was drawn

61

in by it, I didn't understand what was happening to me, and it was only when I began to feel actual physical pain every time you left the room, that it finally dawned on me: I was in love, for the first time in my life. I knew it was hopeless, of course, but that didn't matter to me, because it wasn't like it always had been, it wasn't that I wanted to have you, no. All I wanted was to deserve you. *(MME DE TOURVEL rises decisively to her feet.)*

TOURVEL: I really will have to leave you, Monsieur, you seem determined to persist with a line of argument you must know I ought not to listen to and I don't want to hear.

VALMONT: No, no, please, sit down, sit down. I've already told you, I'll do anything you say. *(Silence. They watch each other. Eventually, MME DE TOURVEL sits down again.)*

TOURVEL: There's only one thing I would like you to do for me.

VALMONT: What? What is it?

TOURVEL: But I don't see how I can ask you, I'm not even sure if I want to put myself in the positon of being beholden to you.

VALMONT: Oh, please, no, I insist, if you're good enough to give me an opportunity to do something you want, anything, it's I who will be beholden to you. *(MME DE TOURVEL looks at VALMONT for a moment with characteristic openness.)*

TOURVEL: Very well, then. I would like you to leave this house. *(There flashes momentarily across VALMONT's face the expression of a chess champion who has just lost his queen.)*

VALMONT: I don't see why that should be necessary.

TOURVEL: Let's just say you've spent your life making it necessary. *(By now, VALMONT has recovered his equilibrium; and thought very fast.)*

VALMONT: Well, then, of course, whatever you say. I couldn't possibly refuse you. *(It's MME DE TOURVEL's turn to be surprised.)* Will you allow me to give my aunt, say, twenty-four hours' notice?

TOURVEL: Well, yes naturally.

VALMONT: I shall find something in my mail tomorrow morning which obliges me to return at once to Paris.

TOURVEL: Thank you, I'd be very grateful.

LES LIAISONS DANGEREUSES

VALMONT: Perhaps I might be so bold as to ask a favour in return. *(MME DE TOURVEL frowns, hesitating.)* I think it would only be just to let me know which of your friends has blackened my name.

TOURVEL: You know very well that's impossible, Monsieur. If friends of mine have warned me against you, they've done so purely in my own interest and I could hardly reward them with betrayal, could I? I must say, you devalue your generous offer if you want to use it as a bargaining point.

VALMONT: Very well, I withdraw the request. I hope you won't think I'm bargaining if I ask you to let me write to you.

TOURVEL: Well...

VALMONT: And hope that you will do me the kindness of answering my letters.

TOURVEL: I'm not sure a correspondence with you is something a woman of honour could permit herself.

VALMONT: So you're determined to refuse all my suggestions, however respectable?

TOURVEL: I really don't see how you could possibly be harmed by conceding me this very minor but, as far as I'm concerned, vitally important consolation.

TOURVEL: I would welcome the chance to prove to you that what motivates me in this is not hatred or resentment, but...

VALMONT: But what? *(But MME DE TOURVEL seems unable to find a statisfactory answer to this. And, moving as suddenly and swiftly as before, VALMONT again crosses the room, drops to one knee and takes her hand. She struggles to free it.)*

TOURVEL: For God's sake, Monsieur, please, leave me alone!

VALMONT: I only want to say what I hardly thought it would be possible for me to say to you: goodbye. *(VALMONT kisses MME DE TOURVEL's hand. She submits briefly, her expression anguished, then begins to struggle again, whereupon he releases her instantly, rises to his feet and bows.)* I'll write soon. *(VALMONT hurries away into the darkness, just failing to muffle a discreet sob. MME DE TOURVEL is left alone, rooted to the chaise-longue. She looks terrified.)*

by Hugh Leonard
Town outside Dublin - Present - Desmond (24) - Mibs (20)

Desmond - A snobbish young intellectual
Mibs - A spunky young woman with a good sense of humor

Serious Desmond is in love with Mibs, a lively young woman
who returns his affection. Desmond's true passion is the
development of the intellect—a pastime for which Mibs lacks
patience and understanding. When Mibs is courted by Lar, a
man of little education, Desmond is hurt by her attration to
someone he feels is his intellectual inferior. Here, Desmond and
Mibs tragically end their love and their friendship.

MIBS: Who let you in?
DESMOND: Your father. He said...well, he seems to be in a temper.
MIBS: *(Toneless.)* That so?
DESMOND: Talk about grumpy: you'd think he was the one with the
toothache. *(He gets no answering smile.)* That friend of yours—
Dorothy Dignam—gave me your message. I was sorry you couldn't
come.
MIBS: When? Oh, to the thingummy.
DESMOND: It was lively enough. I don't know if you'd have enjoyed
it: there was a rough element. It wasn't quite the occasion they'd hoped
for.
MIBS: How was your speech?
DESMOND: Well, I acted the clown, so they laughed a lot. I mean,
if they weren't going to take it seriously, why should I? The history
professor from Trinity, he got a rough time of it. Still, for the
experience—
MIBS: I'm in awful bloody trouble.
DESMOND: ...I daresay it was worth it.
MIBS: I said, I'm in—
DESMOND: I know: I heard you. What kind of trouble?
MIBS: Don't ask me.
DESMOND: Is it...pyorrhoea?

MIBS: No, it's— Is it what?

DESMOND: She said your father was taking you to the dentist.

MIBS: It was to Father Creedon. *(As he stares at her:)* Are you thick? He took me to see old Credo on account of a letter Lar Kearns writ me.

DESMOND: Wrote you. *(Almost laughing.)* Lar Kearns?

MIBS: The first letter he ever writ in his flamin' life, and he sends it to me and me da opens it.

DESMOND: It must have been...worth reading.

MIBS: You shoulda heard old Credo. *(A florid, booming voice:)* "Oh, yass, yass, this is what happens in the house that neglects that grand and glorious Irish custom of the family rosary." Me da was buckin'.

DESMOND: I don't see why.

MIBS: *(Sourly.)* Do you not!

DESMOND: If Kearns's level of prose is anything like his level of conversation, I can imagine the kind of letter it was. That isn't your fault.

MIBS: *(Not answering.)* Do you want tea?

DESMOND: If you like.

MIBS: Might as well. I'm to stay here till I'm called. *(She sets about making tea.)*

DESMOND: Why'd your father open the letter?

MIBS: Becasue I never get any. 'Specially ones with "S.W.A.L.K." on one side and "S.A.G." on the other.

DESMOND: "S.A.G.—?"

MIBS: For "St. Anthony's Guidance." The rotten messer didn't even seal it: he tucked the flap in and put a ha'penny stamp on it.

DESMOND: What did it say?

MIBS: Stuff.

DESMOND: Such as?

MIBS: Things.

DESMOND: Keep it a secret, then.

MIBS: Such a fuss. I went out with a girl I know to Killiney. There was a hop on in the White Cottage, that place on the strand. Lar was at it. He asked me up and bought me a cornet, and at the interval we got two passouts and went up on the bank of the railway.

DESMOND: You and Lar Kearns?

MIBS: God, don't you start.

DESMOND: Well?

MIBS: Well nothing. Mind your own business. Anyway, this morning this letter comes. Writ with a pencil, smelling of mackerel, and all slushy and romantic. *(With an embarrassed laugh:)* Saying he loved me. I mean, Lar Kearns: would you credit it? *(DESMOND is silent.)* And God, doesn't he put in the lot about him and me on the bank of the railway. You'd think I wasn't there and had to be told. It was like the Grand National on the wireless. He even went and put in extra bits: he must have got them out of some book. When I think of me da reading it: all about me creamy breasts. Two "e"s in "creamy" and "b-r-e-s-t," "breasts."

DESMOND: Father Creedon must have enjoyed it.

MIBS: Desmond, he was awful, he ate me. I mean, you'd think we'd done something desperate.

DESMOND: I wouldn't know: I wasn't there. *(The thought of DESMOND being present causes her to giggle.)* Not that I'd want to be.

MIBS: *(On the defensive.)* We had a coort.

DESMOND: Is that what it's called?

MIBS: Well, blast your nerve.

DESMOND: *(Feigning amusement.)* A coort!

MIBS: A bit of messin'. I didn't go all the way with him.

DESMOND: Ah-ha.

MIBS: No, I did not.

DESMOND: Wasn't it dark enough?

MIBS: If you want to know, I nearly did. It was the closest I ever came. Only I wouldn't let him. I wouldn't let anyone. *(He is unmollified. She glares at him, fetches the tea pot and slams it down.)* Because I haven't the nerve. Here.

DESMOND: I don't want your tea.

MIBS: It's bloody made. *(She slushes tea into his cup.)* Me da went down to the harbour to see him...to see Lar, I mean, and give out to

him. *(She puts one spoonful of sugar into his cup.)* How many?
DESMOND: None.
MIBS: Don't stir it. He says he wants to marry me. *(This is what she has been leading up to. She affects to give her attention on putting milk and sugar into her own tea.)* I dunno how he came out with it. I bet you me da waved the letter at him and began rantin' and ravin'. And of course you know Lar. If you said you were starvin' he'd tell you sea-weed was bread and butter. Whatever he thinks you want to hear, that's what he'll say to you, so I suppose he told me da he'd marry me.
DESMOND: In the letter he said he loved you.
MIBS: *(Derisive.)* E-eh.
DESMOND: Well, didn't he?
MIBS: Yeah, because he got a red-hot coort...don't mind him. So now what am I to do?
DESMOND: Marry him.
MIBS: Ah, for God's sake.
DESMOND: Why not?
MIBS: Old jealous-boots.
DESMOND: Who?
MIBS: He hasn't even a proper job. Give over.
DESMOND: Jobs aren't important. I think you should marry him because I think you're his sort.
MIBS: Yeah, the perfect— *(Her smile dies away as the insult goes home.)*
DESMOND: And you won't need a railway bank then, will you, or to be afraid of going all the way with him.
MIBS: Ah, Desmond—
DESMOND: No, you could do worse. I doubt if you'll do better. And you'll be much more your own self at his level than at...anyone else's. *(She realises that he is determined to tear down their relationship past all chance of repair. She starts to clear the tea things.)*
MIBS: Sure. Go on, now: go home.
DESMOND: Mm, it's all hours. I'm sure you'll have a happy life. You'll make a nice home for him, perhaps in one of those cottages in

the Alley Lane. He needs someone like you: you can help him count
his dole money.

MIBS: *(Waiting for him to go.)* Yeah, thanks.

DESMOND: Because—

MIBS: I said, go. You done what you wanted: you said what can't be
took back.

DESMOND: Taken back. *(He is unable to leave ill enough alone. He
wants to draw blood, needs to be certain that her hurt equals his own.)*
I'm very stupid. I mistook you for someone with self-respect. It was
my fault. I thought that at least your ambitions went higher than Lar
Kearns.

MIBS: Do you mean you?

DESMOND: I was wrong.

MIBS: Yes...you do. Well at least Lar is a bit of gas. I can laugh
with him. He's glad of me the way I am. I don't need to have a
scaffolding put around me brain before I'm fit to be seen with him. He
can give a body a coort and a kiss, and they know it's a person, not
bones and cold skin. You think you're so great. Just because you get
up and make a speech and they slap you on the back and cheer you, you
act like you were someone. Well, you're not. They laugh at you. You
have a smell of yourself and you're no one. Honestly, you're not all
there, you know that? The whole town knows about the Drumms. Ask
them. Go and ask. You're as cracked as your oul' fella was. I'm not
surprised he went and— *(She breaks off.)*

DESMOND: That he went and what?

MIBS: Go on home.

DESMOND: Yes.

MAIDS OF HONOR
by Joan Casademont
Suburban Boston - Present - Monica (30's) - Roger (30's)

Monica - A talk show hostess and bride-to-be
Roger - Monica's ex-lover

Three sisters; Monica, Izzy and Annie, have gathered at their family home for Monica's wedding to a stock broker of questionable morality. Here, Monica's former lover, Roger, confronts her about her coming marriage to her crooked fiance.

ROGER: Is there someplace—a little more private where we could talk?

MONICA: No.

ROGER: Good start, Monica. Good start.

MONICA: Make it fast, Roger. I have a ceremony to attend. *(Pause. ROGER comes further into the room, leans on a counter, exhausted.)*

ROGER: I'm sorry I overslept, I got here last night.

MONICA: You weren't invited.

ROGER: You seem a little rattled.

MONICA: *(Hardly looking at him)* You look like shit.

ROGER: Thanks.

MONICA: Anytime. *(Pause.)*

ROGER: Monica, I think we should just stop all the bullshit and just plunge in and get married.

MONICA: What?

ROGER: Married. You and me.

MONICA: *(With a laugh)* Roger, I'm already getting married. That's what this ceremony is today, it's a wedding ceremony. There's a tent the size of Texas in the backyard. I'm wearing a wedding dress. Note the white?

ROGER: Please don't talk to me like that. Please, Monica, gimme a fuckin' break.

MONICA: Well, I'm just a little amazed. I mean, talk about waiting until the last minute.

ROGER: When you get that tone with me, you know I start shouting

69

even though I don't want to. I told myself today that no matter what
happened, no matter what you said to me, I would not shout.

MONICA: Well, aren't I the lucky one today! I'm gonna be treated
like a dog.

ROGER: Neither of us would abuse a dog the way we abuse each
other, Monica, and it's gonna stop. It's gonna stop right now. *(Pause.
MONICA crosses to the table, sits.)*

MONICA: I can't believe you came.

ROGER: Neither can I.

MONICA: You drove the whole way?

ROGER: Yup.

MONICA: Where'd you stay.

ROGER: Some—Inn up the street. Heard you got bad news last night.
This guy's a crook?

MONICA: *(With a shrug)* Guess so.

ROGER: Why would you wanna marry a crook.

MONICA: I don't know. Makes me feel protected. *(Pause.)*

ROGER: You're such a blockhead. I'm sorry I didn't come to your
birthday party. I'm sorry I lose my temper and call you a bitch and I'm
sorry I shouted at you in front of the moving men.

MONICA: I'm sorry for everything. I am a bitch.

ROGER: Oh, you're not that bad.

MONICA: I'm sorry I abandoned you. I guess I should've warned
you first.

ROGER: *(Dissolving, coming over to embrace her with open arms.)*
Oh, Monica! Ho-ney! We can make it, can't we? Now we're getting
somewhere. Aren't we getting somewhere here?

MONICA: *(Jumping up, pulling away from him)* No, Roger, no! I
mean, we always get somewhere and then everything just busts apart,
it just goes flyin' all around! You're too late. Do you understand?
You're just too late. *(Pause. ROGER takes a moment, and then
decisively pulls something out of his pocket. It is a ring, a gold
wedding band. HE wipes it off, tries to give it to her.)*

ROGER: Here.

MONICA: *(Not taking it)* What is that.

MAIDS OF HONOR

ROGER: A ring.

MONICA: *(With a laugh)* I already have a ring. Sorry, Roger, but I have a real ring. See? *(SHE shows him the ring. HE puts his on the table.)*

ROGER: This one's better.

MONICA: God, Roger, you are unbelievable! We sat there for hours—humiliating ourselves in front of that doctor, you talking endlessly about how we should just get engaged, not get married for another year, not have kids until we were about a hundred, and now you expect me to just jump at this pathetic little carrot on the same day that I am supposed to marry someone else, someone who is really there for me?!

ROGER: You don't give two shits about this guy, and he is certainly not there for you.

MONICA: He is so! You don't know anything about it.

ROGER: After all we've been through together, the fact that you can look me in the eye and lie about some—prop of a guy makes me just wanna—

MONICA: Smack me?

ROGER: Throw up!

MONICA: Oh! What a delightful image.

ROGER: I'm breaking this fucked up pattern, Monica! I'm not playin' any games anymore, I'm gonna jump right in and marry you today if you want! Right now, right here, we can get married in that fuckin' tent, you and me, like we should have a long time ago.

MONICA: Oh, you are ridiculous!

ROGER: *(Shouts)* STOP IT, MONICA! STOP FUCKING ABUSING ME SO I CAN ABUSE YOU BACK! *(Pause. MONICA runs to the door, frightened. IZZY and ANNIE react outside, on alert, but don't come in.)*

MONICA: Please don't shout at me, Roger. Please don't shout.

ROGER: I'm not gonna shout! No matter what you say to me. I'm not gonna shout!

MONICA: God, I am totally lost.

ROGER: Then stop fighting it, Monica! Stop believing I'm gonna turn into your father because I raise my voice! I'm just like you, I have problems, I'm wounded, I'm scared to death, but I can get over it, I'm gonna get over it! If we keep at it, we can still get over it together, can't we? *(Pause.)* Will you marry me, Monica? Please? Pretty please? *(MONICA moves away, circles the table so that it is between them. Pause.)*

MONICA: No.

ROGER: No? Why not?

MONICA: You're not asking me in a very romantic way.

ROGER: Oh, for Christ's sake! What do you want from me? You moved out on me! It took everything I had to come here! I'm trying as hard as I can, please, what do you want from me?

MONICA: Unconditional, unequivocal, total acceptance and love. Something you will never be able to give to me.

ROGER: Oh, Monica! I'm not your fuckin' Daddy!

MONICA: Well I certainly didn't get that from him.

ROGER: I mean I cannot be the parent you never had, I'm just a person with a past, I'm not a saint!

MONICA: Maybe the wrong past, maybe both our pasts together are just totally impossible to manage.

ROGER: You want a concept, not a person! Only Monica, this fuckin' banker guy is eventually gonna make you even more miserable!

MONICA: Maybe.

ROGER: Yes! You know that—thing, that step Doctor Mellman kept talking about? Like that we were like two five-year-olds on a diving board going, 'you go first,' 'no, you go first', 'no, you go first'?, so no one went first so no one ever got to experience how exhilarating it might be to just dive into the water and come up floating and supported?

MONICA: I hated that woman's imagery. All I kept thinking was, yeah, fine, but what if somebody forgot to fill the pool?

ROGER: There is water in the pool, Monica. She was right about this. Besides, I'm telling you, I'm diving in first, so I'll break my head if there's no water in the pool, but I'm not worried, because there's water in the pool! *(Pause.)*

MONICA: What about kids. Do we still have to be a hundred? I'm thirty-three, Roger. I'm already thirty-three years old.

ROGER: We should still wait on that one.

MONICA: Wait? How long?

ROGER: Couple of years.

MONICA: But I can't wait a couple of years, that's impossible, that's just impossible. *(Pause.)* I'm sorry, Roger, the answer just has to be no. Now I have a ceremony to attend if you'll excuse me. Thank you for—well, thank you for coming.

(SHE goes to the steps. IZZY, hearing this exchange, comes close to the screen door. ANNIE tries to stop her but IZZY pulls away. IZZY waits at the door, unseen.)

ROGER: 'Thank you for coming?!' What the hell, did you just turn into a stewardess or something?

MONICA: Roger, I cannot wait to have children. Do you understand, I can not wait! *(Pause.)*

ROGER: Are you telling me you're pregnant?

MONICA: Yes.

ROGER: With his kid.

MONICA: *(Not looking at him.)* Yes.

ROGER: You're positive it's his.

MONICA: Yes. *(Pause.)*

ROGER: How long.

MONICA: Couple months.

ROGER: Couple months? Like eight weeks?

MONICA: More.

ROGER: How much more.

MONICA: Enough!

ROGER: Jesus, Monica. Was it an accident?

MONICA: Yes.

ROGER: Is it really too late to stop it?

MONICA: *(Shouts)* I cannot and will not have an abortion! *(Pause.)*

ROGER: Well I don't know what the hell to say. I don't know why the hell you took that chance except to just get back at me.

MONICA: Good-bye, Roger.

ROGER: You still don't have to marry the guy.

MIRIAM'S FLOWERS
by Migdalia Cruz
Bronx - Present - Miriam (16) - Enrique (20's)

Miriam - A young girl driven to self-mutilation by the death of
      her brother
Enrique - Miriam's lover

Puli's death has driven Miriam to many extreme acts and now
she has managed to seduce Enrique, the owner of the local
grocery store. Here she convinces Enrique to allow her to carve
flowers into his arm with a razor blade as she does to herself.

(MIRIAM and ENRIQUE in MIRIAM's apartment. ENRIQUE is on top
of her.)
MIRIAM: Dead animals are very interesting. I mean, unless you're
a scientist or somefin, you don' get to see an animal's insides like that.
You know what's interesting? How crows eat other crows. What's the
matter wif those crows? Or are they right? Are we supposed to go off
eating all our dead relatives?
ENRIQUE: I don't know... I don't think so.
MIRIAM: You don't think so? —I don' either. Birds are weird
things. They got those weird toes and those weird beaks. I don' like
the looks of them at all. It's not natural.
ENRIQUE: That's for sure... My mother keeps birds.
MIRIAM: What kind?
ENRIQUE: Six parakeets and one parrot and the parrot don't fly.
MARIAM: What's he do then?
ENRIQUE: He walks. Mostly backwards. And if you let him out of
the cage, he crawls along the side of the wall like a spy or something.
And gets into the cracks in the wall and wedges himself behind the sofa.
He stayed back there for three days once.
MIRIAM: It's a miracle he din't die.
ENRIQUE: Ma said he lived on roaches. She seen him go after them
when they're inside his cage. He likes them... I mean, I don't
understand it, but I'm no bird.
MIRIAM: No, you're not no bird alright.

MIRIAM'S FLOWERS

ENRIQUE: Not no fucking bird.

MIRIAM: Roaches, huh? You ever actually seen him swallow one?

ENRIQUE: Sure.

MIRIAM: Did it make you want to throw up?

ENRIQUE: No.

MIRIAM: It makes me sick even to think about it...but you know, I bet they taste kind of sweet.

ENRIQUE: Yeah?

MIRIAM: You know why I think that? Because they are always in the sweets. Walking around in sugar, trying to get into the sweet grease in the gas holes of the oven...

ENRIQUE: Yeah...

MIRIAM: And when you turn on the oven, you hear that crackling sound, but not all of them die. Their little asses are burning, but they made it out. *(Pause)* It's like this dream I had about these alligator women... They was coming here, to the Bronx to get me and take me out... And I almos' went wif 'em too, but they wouldn't let me take my statue of San Martin de Porres. And I don'go nowhere wifout him.

ENRIQUE: Is that all you got for me? Your stupid dreams? C'mon. Let's do...you know, it.

MIRIAM: Who's stopping you?

ENRIQUE: I know all about you. About what kind of girl you are. You take your panties off for everybody else—why not for me?

MIRIAM: I can't spread my legs no more... I'm too tired to hold them apart.

ENRIQUE: I'll hold them open for you.

MIRIAM: Go home. You have a wife.

ENRIQUE: She's dead—down there I mean.

MIRIAM: You don'even know what to call it.

ENRIQUE: Papaya.. Sweet Guava... Honeyed tropical fruit. The kind that pulls out your fillings. So sweet it hurts.

MIRIAM: You shouldn't do nuffin that makes you hurt.

ENRIQUE: I'm hurting now. *(HE takes her hand and puts it on his crotch)* See?

MIRIAM: *(Pulling her hand away)* Shit. It feels like a blackjack.

MIRIAM'S FLOWERS

ENRIQUE: Wanna see?

MIRAIM: Go home.

ENRIQUE: You'll never have to pay for razors again. I'll order the kind you like—blue with the swords.

MIRIAM: I'll paint you a picture... Close your eyes. *(HE does so and SHE takes out a razor and begins to cut lightly into his arm.)*

ENRIQUE: Are you crazy?!

MIRIAM: It'll only hurt a little bit.

ENRIQUE: I don't care how much it hurts! You're not cuttin' into my arm.

MIRIAM: What are you scared of? *(SHE begins to unbutton her blouse.)*

ENRIQUE: You shouldn't do that. You're gonna get sick. You could poison your blood like that. What do you do that for?

MIRIAM: For fun.

ENRIQUE: Fun? We was having fun before you cut me.

MIRIAM: You like me, don't you? *(SHE takes off her blouse)* It's gonna be a real pretty picture.

ENRIQUE: Oh, God! You're so beautiful. *(SHE takes his hands and puts them on her breasts.)* You're so soft, baby. Let me taste you. Let me put my tongue inside you...

MIRIAM: It'll hurt really good... Close you eyes. *(HE closes his eyes and nervously hands her his arm.)*

ENRIQUE: Just a little bit, okay. *(SHE carves a heart into his arm.)*

MIRIAM: It's like the sacred heart of Jesus. Look at it.

ENRIQU: Lydia's not gonna like this.

MIRIAM: Sure. I'll just put her name through the middle of it...then she'll love you forever.

ENRIQUE: *(Gasping, as SHE cuts into his arm.)* Ay! Uhhh, maybe just an "L", okay?

ONE-ACT PLAY
by Yannick Murphy
Rural America - Present - Ray (20's) - Alix (13)

Ray - A young man who has locked himself in his mother's
   bedroom
Alix - Ray's younger sister

Ray and Alix must each come to grips with being abondoned by
their father. Ray has locked himself in his mother's bedroom,
refusing to come out. Here, Alix attempts to pursuade Ray to
come out and eat something.

*(Alix steps back inside the house. Walks around the room a little, then
runs the brush through her own hair. She goes up to the door that
Ray's behind and listens against it. Then she walks around the room
again. Out loud and non-chalantly she begins to talk.)*
ALIX: We only got bread.
(Ray speaks from inside the door.)
RAY: I know that.
ALIX: Well ain't you hungry yet?
RAY: Go get me somthin', Alix.
ALIX: I think you're an asshole.
RAY: She broke the guitar.
ALIX: I would if I was her too.
RAY: Don't be sayin' this 'cause you think I can't come out and hit
you. 'Cause I can come out any goddamn time I want to.
ALIX: So come out and hit me.
RAY: And don't even think about bringin' Linda here.
ALIX: I forgot, we got some Murphy Noodle Soup too.
RAY: We always got Murphy Noodle Soup.
ALIX: She made some new yesterday though, right after you took over
her room.
RAY: I didn't take over her room.
ALIX: Yeah, well then how come she can't get in there?
RAY: Just shut up.
ALIX: Have you gone through the mail yet?

77

RAY: I haven't been outta here since yesterday stupid. I'm gettin' hungry. You get me somethin'?

ALIX: Just because you're sore at her you better not be hidin' things from me. Don't be hidin' my mail on me. I'm gonna set up shop soon, in front of Garsha's. He said if I paid him I could rent out the block in front of his door. That way I'd get all the customers goin' into his place. But first he wants to see my license.

RAY: What the hell are you talkin' about?

ALIX: They sent me a test in the mail, it had all these pages with palms drawn on them, palms with real lines like you'd find on your own hands, life lines and stuff and I interpreted it all, as if it were a real hand. Now they're supposed to send me my certification. So I can ask for money in a legal way. I'm gonna learn divinin' too.

RAY: Yeah? You gonna be takin' swimmin' lessons? *(He laughs to himself.)*

ALIX: No, asshole, I said divinin', not divin'.

RAY: Lexy, listen, will you pour me some of the soup?

ALIX: Yeah? Then what? You want me to pour it through the keyhole so you can stand on the other side with your ugly mouth hangin' open?

RAY: No, you come to the door and I'll open it just wide enough to take the bowl from you.

ALIX: *(Shaking her head.)* Uh-uh. You know Mama can't stand to have people eatin' in the bedroom. She'd break your face if you did that.

RAY: Well she ain't here now.

ALIX: We only got two bowls, and I'm not gonna tell her I broke one or somethin' just to cover you.

RAY: We got more mugs though, pour it into two mugs for me.

ALIX: If I do will you let me read your palm?

RAY: Oh Lexy, you've read my palm a million times, I swear my lines are gonna disappear by the time you're done tracin' your fingers over them. Then I'm gonna be a nobody. A man without fingerprints ain't no man at all Alix.

ALIX: I don't give shit about your fingerprints. It's your palms that

ONE-ACT PLAY

I look at.

RAY: O.K., but don't tell me what it says this time, 'cause I'm sick of it already. I know it by heart.

(Alix goes to refrigerator, pulls out a pot with a tin foil lid, lights the stove, and heats the soup.)

ALIX: No, that's the part that counts when I'm practicin', I got to make them believe with my voice that I'm tellin' the truth. You've got to let me talk it out!

RAY: But it ain't the truth, honey. I never married Linda. We ain't never gonna have three kids, one of em's gonna be a doctor, none of that's gonna happen. I'm never gonna win the lottery or own a red truck. You just say those things 'cause you want them to happen. I know you like the color red Alix.

ALIX: You and Linda are gonna get back together again. Your palm says it so loud that my fingertips hurt from it everytime. You two are gonna get married. I already picked out my red dress for the weddin'. I know it's in October. The trees are gonna be lit up in orange and red, instead of people throwin' rice, they'll be throwin' October leaves at you and Linda. Mama promised me she'd wear an orange dress, so we'd look good together. *(Pause)* Ray, you listenin'? You ought to cause it's the honest to God truth. Linda's gonna be back. She owes me and Mama that much anyway. I'll tell you somethin' though, last time I saw you, you looked pale, you need a vacation. You need time to gain back your confidence.

RAY: Where am I gonna go Lexy? You see that in my palm too?

ALIX: I think you should go up to Sugarloaf. Borrow someone's tent and then get up real early in the mornin', pull aside the flaps of that tent and stand up by the drop off, and look down at Warwick Valley and think to yourself, I've been there before and I know it all, and it's good and it's home.

RAY: Lexy, honey, you go look and tell me how bad off that guitar is. I heard her put it in the closet.

(Alix goes to closet, pulls out guitar and lays it on the kitchen table.)

ALIX: Neck's about to come off, Ray. Looks like that pup Wicca had, that retard pup we called Goofey, looks like that Ray, like

ONE-ACT PLAY

Goofey—who couldn't hold his head up.

RAY: What do you think? Think I can fix it?

ALIX: No prayer.

RAY: She thinks I can forget about her. She says time's gonna heal everything up, like a big patch that you iron on your jeans. I want to laugh when she talks like that cause then she goes and breaks that guitar, like she's gonna get him out of her blood once and for all. Showin' me that if she can do it then I can do it too. But then she says it was her first birthday gift from him, and that you don't forget those things.

ALIX: Wicca ate that pup. They say the mother knows when the pup's a bad one, so they eat it. To me that's really somethin', makes me wonder why they have that retard house over in Goshen, like what for? Besides, Mama just says it wastes tax money. Beth Winson told me retards don't have no fingerprints, 'cause they've got nothin' on their minds. I'd like to see one of their palms.

RAY: I've been lookin' in her mirror. I keep tryin' to tell myself what she tells me to. But my eye keeps wanderin' to this picture that's wedged in the side of her mirror. She's standin' in the forest, by the lake, she's wearin' his lumber jacket, it's way too big for her, but she looks happy in it, like it's full of his smell or somethin', and it just pleases her no end to be wearin' it. Then I hear her through the door tellin' me this whole thing's gonna blow over, that I'll forget about Linda, meanwhile the pictures got be over twenty years old and it's right next to the hairbrush she uses everyday. If he found out she broke that guitar he'd probably kill her.

ALIX: He ain't comin' back. He ain't gonna kill her. He ain't like her. He don't hold onto things. He never could remember when her birthday was anyway.

RAY: Lexy you think palm lines ever change?

ALIX: What?

RAY: Do they ever grow, or go off in another direction as you get older?

ALIX: I never read anythin' like that before. It doesn't seem like it though. Seems like what you're born with is what you're stuck with.

80

Like half the time you think a decision you made one day was your
very own, but it wasn't, it's all written down for you on your hands the
day you're born. That's why it's somethin' I got to do. I've got to
give people a little control over their lives. If you know what's comin'
you feel better. Everybody's lookin' for control. The only way they're
gonna get it is if they look at their hands. If Mama knew he was gonna
leave her, like her palm says, then she wouldda asked for a Baby
Grand, not no Goya. I only regret not bein' there to tell her.
RAY: Yeah, but it's the sound of the guitar she always liked the best.

THE PINK STUDIO
by Jane Anderson
France - 1900's - Henri (40-50) - Claudine (40's)

Henri Matisse - A famous artist
Claudine - Henri's strong-willed wife

Well aware of her husband's philandering ways, Claudine
Matisse proves to be more than a match for him as she describes
an evening that she spent out on the town in order to punish him
for abandoning her.

*(We are in the lobby of the hotel. Claudine is sitting on a chair in a
yellow party dress, waiting for Henri.)*
HENRI: Claudine!
CLAUDINE: Hello, Henri.
HENRI: Where have you been? I've been worried sick. I called the
police.
CLAUDINE: Didn't you get my note?
HENRI: Yes, but it didn't say you'd be gone all night.
CLAUDINE: I told you not to wait up for me. I thought you'd be
sound asleep. You know how you are when you've been out with
Andre.
HENRI: I wasn't asleep. I was pacing the room. I was wretched.
(the dress) What is this? What are you wearing? Is that how you were
all night?
CLAUDINE: Yes.
HENRI: What were you doing?
CLAUDINE: I'll tell you. *(The waitress, LUCILLE, enters with a
breakfast tray. She sets rolls and coffee on the table and a small vase
with carnations.)* How nice. Carnations.
HENRI: I bought you flowers, you know. I was going to have them
waiting for you in the room. But you were gone so long they died and
I had to throw them away.
CLAUDINE: Oh really? How long were you out before you put them
in water? *(Claudine takes a seat at the table.)*
HENRI: Did you do this to punish me?

82

THE PINK STUDIO

CLAUDINE: Not at all.

HENRI: Tell me where you went.

CLAUDINE: I went shopping.

HENRI: Shopping?

CLAUDINE: Yes. Andre suggested it, don't you remember?

HENRI: No. You went shopping all night?

CLAUDINE: No... *(Claudine takes a long sip of her coffee.)*

HENRI: For God sakes, what? Tell me what you did.

CLAUDINE: After you and Andre left, I went for a walk. I decided that the best thing I could be doing at the moment was spending your money.

HENRI: Fine, I deserved it. And where did you go?

CLAUDINE: I went into a dress shop. And a gentleman there wanted me to try on a dress.

HENRI: What? How perverse! Who was he?

CLAUDINE: He was a designer. Jean Patou.

HENRI: I've never heard of him.

CLAUDINE: He's very well known.

HENRI: I don't know him.

CLAUDINE: He happened to be in the shop and he wanted someone to model one of his new designs. For some reason my figure caught his eye.

HENRI: Why was he doing this?

CLAUDINE: I don't know. I didn't care. I was having a marvelous time.

HENRI: Then what?

CLAUDINE: He got out a box of pins and made adjustments on the dress. He said "Your figure is perfect for the dress but the dress is not yet perfect for your figure."

HENRI: Did he try to touch you?

CLAUDINE: I don't recall. And then, let's see, he took me next door to a coiffeuse and told her how to do my hair. She was very impressed. She gave me champagne and treated me to a pedicure.

HENRI: A pedicure?

(Claudine slips off a shoe and wiggles her toes at Henri.)

THE PINK STUDIO

CLAUDINE: See?

HENRI: Where are your stockings?

CLAUDINE: *(not answering)* So about an hour later, this Monsieur Patou came back with this hat.

HENRI: Claudine, what happened to your stockings?

CLAUDINE: Perhaps I left them at the shop. *(going on)* He said that we needed the wide brim of the hat to offset the flair of the dress. He said that everything we wear must have a balance of shapes.

HENRI: Oh, please! Any amateur learns that the first week of art class.

CLAUDINE: Fine, Henri. But I have to tell you, when I saw myself in the mirror I was amazed by how striking I looked.

HENRI: Haven't I told you that? Haven't I told you for years that you're a magnificent creature?

CLAUDINE: Yes you have.

HENRI; I'm at a loss, Claudine. All these years I've been trying to put my love for you on the canvas and you tell me that you've gotten nothing from this.

CLAUDINE: That's not what I said.

HENRI: You let some stranger put you in a yellow dress covered with bows that look like dying moths. I'm at a loss.

CLAUDINE: But Henri, a painting is an expression of you, not of me.

HENRI: You don't think this Patou was using you like a canvas?

CLAUDINE: And what if he was? I love the dress. It makes me feel stunning.

HENRI: Then what am I painting for? Why don't I just learn how to sew? I'll throw away my brushes open up the House of Henri.

CLAUDINE: You're a painter, Henri, it's not your job to make women feel beautiful. When I pose for you I do it because you ask me to and because I'm happy to help you in your work. But I certainly don't do it for my own pleasure. But when you're done and you show me the painting it's more often than not quite brilliant. But does it make me feel like a masterpiece myself? If it did, my love, you wouldn't have to pay your models. They would be paying you. So stop being hurt.

HENRI: So, then what happened, after you put on this dress and it changed your life.

CLAUDINE: Oh stop, it didn't change my life.

HENRI: What happened then?

CLAUDINE: Well, Patou wanted me to join him for dinner. I said I couldn't because I was going to dine with you. Then I came back here and waited for you for three hours.

HENRI: Three hours? I was only an hour late.

CLAUDINE; Oh please. So I rang him up and said I'd be dining with him after all.

HENRI: So you went to dinner?

CLAUDINE: Yes.

HENRI: And then?

CLAUDINE: We drove to Monte Carlo.

HENRI: What, in his car?

CLAUDINE: Yes.

HENRI: What for?

CLAUDINE: I don't know, Henri, it was something to do.

HENRI: And then?

CLAUDINE: We drove back and watched the sun rise over the ocean. Then I came up to have breakfast with you.

HENRI; And what happened to your stockings?

CLAUDINE: Perhaps I left them on the beach.

HENRI: I see.

(Claudine pours some more coffee for herself.)

CLAUDINE: And what did you do with your day? Did you and Andre see Maurice?

HENRI: Yes.

CLAUDINE: Did you see his new work?

HENRI: Yes.

CLAUDINE: And how is it?

HENRI: Derivative.

CLAUDINE: Oh.

HENRI: Are you going to see this man again?

CLAUDINE: No.

HENRI: But you're keeping the dress?
CLAUDINE: Yes, of course. What do you want me to do, burn it?
HENRI: I really don't care. *(A beat.)* Will you pose for me?
CLAUDINE: Right now?
HENRI: Yes. I'd like to paint you in the dress.
CLAUDINE: I'm too tired to sit for you right now.
HENRI: Please, Claudine.
(Claudine pats his hand.)
CLAUDINE: My love, it's all right. I'm sure whatever you paint will be far more brilliant than the dress. But you don't need to prove that to me right now. I'm going up to change. Then I'm going down to the beach. Why don't you meet me in the cabana? We can take a nap.
HENRI: A nap?
CLAUDINE: *(smiling)* Or not.

PRELUDE TO A KISS
by Craig Lucas
New York City - Present - Peter (20-30) - Rita (20-30)

Peter - A microfiche specialist
Rita - The woman Peter loves

Peter and Rita have fallen in love and here they tentatively explore their feelings for one another.

(Rita's apartment.)
PETER: This is great.
RITA: You want a Molsen?
PETER: You drink Molsen—
RITA: Uh-huh.
PETER: —in your own home?
RITA: I've been known to.
PETER; That's really...
RITA: A coincidence.
PETER: A coincidence. So why can't you sleep? I want to solve this.
RITA: I really wasn't exaggerating. It's been since I was fourteen.
PETER: That's a lot of journal keeping... Have you seen doctors?
RITA: I've seen all the doctors.
PETER: Uh-huh.
RITA: Of every know...
PETER: Right.
RITA: *(overlapping)* Persuasion. I've ingested countless... *(SHE hands him a Molsen.)*
PETER: Thanks.
RITA: Pills, liquids, I've seen an acupuncturist.
PETER: You did? What did it feel like?
RITA: Little needles in your back.
PETER: It hurt?
RITA: Sometimes.
PETER: They always lie.
RITA: I know.
PETER: You're really beautiful. *(SHE laughs.)* You are.

87

PRELUDE TO A KISS

RITA: Thank you. That's... No, thank you.

(THEY kiss. SHE laughs.)

PETER: This is not supposed to be the funny part.

RITA: No, I know, I'm sorry... I'm, I guess I'm nervous.

PETER: Why are you nervous? Don't be nervous.

RITA: All right.

(HE approaches to kiss her.)

PETER: Don't laugh... All right, you can laugh. *(THEY kiss.)* Am I going too fast? *(SHE shakes her head.)* Is this tacky of me? *(Headshake.)* Oh good. *(THEY kiss.)* This is definitely the highlight of my weekend. *(SHE smiles.)* So maybe we should just, you know, watch some TV, have happy memories of this and anticipate the future— *(SHE is shaking her head.)* —we shouldn't? *(THEY kiss.)* I would really, really like to see you with all of your clothes off and stuff like that.

RITA: I would really, really like to see you with all of your clothes off and...

PETER: Stuff like that?

THE SECRET SITS IN THE MIDDLE
by Lisa-Marie Radano
Coney Island - Present - Tina (20's) - Sonny (20's)

Tina - A young woman seeking an abortion
Sonny - Tina's lover

When Tina finds out that she is pregnant, she immediately decides to have an abortion. Here, she is sitting in the waiting room of the clinic when Sonny bursts in and tries to stop her.

SONNY: You been bad.

TINA: Oh yea?

SONNY: Yea. You went and told Angie before me. Now you must be punished.

TINA: Gee. Look how I'm shaken. Whatya gonna do ta me?

SONNY: It starts with first you gotta come over here and sit in my lap.

TINA: Sonny. Ain't you got no regard for a public place?

SONNY: Yea. I like the Grand Canyon. But my lap is very nice too. And you don't gotta share it with the Japanese.

TINA: We gotta talk first.

SONNY: OK. But first get over here.

TINA: No. You know what's gonna happen if I come over there. You'll start doin all that stuff you do ta my neck which makes me point my toes and gasp for air.

SONNY: You KNOW if I come over there it'll be much worse for ya. But since I love ya I'll be a gent and give ya five.

SONNY: You smell nice. Just like Chips Ahoy.

TINA: Cut it out. You're getten me breathen.

SONNY: I was once a lifeguard.

(Sonny sticks his face into Tina's chest. He makes growling noises.)

TINA: Sonny. That's really nice—but it hurts like a tetnus shot.

SONNY: I'm massagen your heart wit my face. It's a life-saven technique.

TINA: Quit goofen around!

SONNY: You know I never tickled a pregnant woman before. Except maybe my Ma, but that was internal so it don't count.

TINA: Don't you dare.

THE SECRET SITS IN THE MIDDLE

SONNY: Where's that rib I love so much?

TINA: Don't. JUST don't. Don't even consider it! Don't? Don't?

(Sonny pokes and jabs Tina's ribs. She is very ticklish.)

TINA: Cut it out Sonny! I'm gonna puke on you!

SONNY: You puke! Ha! You ain't puked since the first day-a Kindergarden.

TINA: Yea. And my teacher was wearen new pumps!

SONNY: Watch. I don't even gotta touch ya to be touchen ya.

(He holds his hand just above Tina's ribcage and lets it just crawl in the air. This drives Tina crazy, she starts giggling, Sonny starts tickling her again.)

TINA: Quit it Sonny!

SONNY: Almost. Just a few more seconds.

TINA: STOP IT!!!

(Tina struggles and in a burst of strength she elbows Sonny sharply in the lower gut. She gets up and goes back to the couch. Sonny gasps for air.)

SONNY: *(Winded)* Whatsa matter with you? You got the mood?

TINA: NO! I ain't got the flippen mood! When you're pregnant you don't get the mood because you don't get the thing, you dope.

SONNY: Well gahead and explain it ta me Miss Registered Nurse.

TINA: Look I don't know how it all works. It's gotta do with chemicals so I don't give a care. I just wanna get in there and get it over with.

SONNY: What?

TINA: You know that. Whatya think we're sitten here waiten for?

SONNY: For the soda?

TINA: Jesus Sonny! Whatya got in ya head? A brain or a roll-a tape?

SONNY: OK! You reached me now! I hadda bouta nuffa you today! Alla these little snips and snipes like I'm only a lamp inna room without no feelings. Tell me—who the fuck do you think you are, THE KENNEDIES?

TINA: Don't yell at me! I'm scared enough as it is!

SONNY: For whatya scared?

TINA: Whatya mean what ya stupid jerk? YOU don't have-ta go in there where it's all bad smells and bright overhead lights peelen your skin slowly in a way you can't feel and strangers touchen your body

90

inna bad way. Inna way you shouldn't ever BE touched! Like the way a butcher lifts up a wingofa chicken. That's how they touch, like they never loved nothen, not even a fish inna bowl. It's supposed ta be quick. But then they keep me waiting out here for fucking ever! DO THEY WANT ME TA SUFFER?

SONNY: We're in one-a those places...where they do those things?

TINA: It's a clinic. Don't act like it's hades.

SONNY: You were gonna get a...thing?

TINA: Don't get all choked.

SONNY: You were! You weren't even gonna tell me. Angela told me. Angela cared. If it weren't for Angela, I'd be washen cars and you'd be here haven a...thing.

TINA: Come sit nexta me.

SONNY: I can barely look at ya.

TINA: It's my body!

SONNY: It's my baby!

TINA: No. No it ain't. It ain't a baby yet.

SONNY: What is it then? You tell me that? If it ain't a baby, what is it then—an oven mitt?

TINA: Nobody knows that. That's why they keep doin talk shows about it. Because they don't know.

SONNY: So you woulda just done it. What could I do ta stop you? Nothen. You got all a the power. Me—alls I did was sink the basket and now I'm like—benched. Biology. It's cruel.

TINA: You're no fucken help. You're acten like a little baby boy.

SONNY: Well I'm not a little boy. I'M THE FATHER!

TINA: Now I'm impressed.

SONNY: Yeah! I'm a Father! I AM SOMETHING IN THIS!

TINA: Shut up.

SONNY: I'M A FATHER! And you—YOU'RE A MOTHER! GET UP! *(He grabs the upper part of her arm.)*

TINA: Angela?!?

SONNY: Get up! We're getten outa here! *(He pulls her to her feet.)*

TINA: You maybe. I'm stayen. Angela!!

SONNY: We got things ta talk about. You and me! MOTHER AND FATHER!

TINA: ANGELA!?! HELP!!!

SPEED-THE-PLOW
by David Mamet
Hollywood - Present - Gould (40's) - Karen (20's)

Gould - A movie producer
Karen - Gould's temporary secretary

Charlie Fox brings his boss, Bobby Gould, a hot script that one of Hollywoods's top director's dropped on his lap. A potential money-maker, replete with sex and violence. In order to get Karen over to his place to seduce her, Gould has given her an "arty" script to read. Karen, who is not as naive as she seems, has ambitions of her own.

GOULD: You've done a fantastic job.
KAREN: I have?
GOULD: Yes.
KAREN: I have? Doing what?
GOULD: On the book. *(pause)*
KAREN: I...?
GOULD: In your report on the book. It means something, it means a lot, I want to tell you, if you want to "do" something out here. A *freshness*, you said a *naiveté*, but call it a "freshness," and a capacity to get involved...I think that it's fantastic. And, you know, you dream about making a connection; but I feel I've *done* it.
KAREN: You've made a connection...
GOULD: Yes. And you reached out to *me*.
KAREN: I did...
GOULD: You shared this thing with me.
KAREN: ...the book...
GOULD: You did it. Someone does something...*totally*...
KAREN: ...yes...
GOULD: And you say "yes"... "*That's*...that's what I've been missing."
KAREN: ...you're saying...
GOULD: That's what I've been missing. I'm saying, you come *alive*, and you say everyone's been holding their *breath* in this town, twenty

years, forever, *I* don't know...and then...

KAREN: Yes...

GOULD: So rare, someone shows, shows some *enthusiasm*...it becomes, it becomes *simple*. You know what I mean...

KAREN: Yes. I do.

GOULD: N'I want to thank you. (pause)

KAREN: Um...it's nothing.

GOULD: *(simultaneously with "nothing")* It's something. No. Let, let, let, let me *help* you. That's what I want to do.

KAREN: *(pause)* I'm confused.

GOULD: I'm saying I *thank* you; I want to do something for you.

KAREN: No, no...

GOULD: And whatever, I'm saying, if I can, that you would like to do, in, in the *studio*, if you would like to do it, if I can help you with it, then I would like to help you.

KAREN: Yes. *Thank* you. *(pause)* I absolutely do. You *know* what I want to do.

GOULD: I...?

KAREN: I want to work on the film.

GOULD: Alright. If we can. The *Prison* film...

KAREN: No. On this. *This* film. The *Radiation* film and I don't care. I don't care in what capacity, well, why *should* I, 'cause I don't have any skills...*that's* presumptuous, of *course*, in any way I could. But I'd just like, it would be so important to me to *be* there. To help. *(pause)* If you could just help me with that. And, seriously, I'll get coffee, I don't care, but if you could do that for me, I would be... *(pause)*

GOULD: Hmmm.

KAREN: I've put you on the spot.

GOULD: No. Yes, a little.

KAREN: I'm serious. I'd do *anything*...

GOULD: *(pause)* Look... *(pause)* This was a "courtesy read."

KAREN: I know that, but...

GOULD: As I told you, the chances were, were astronomically slim that it would...

SPEED-THE-PLOW

KAREN: Of course, but you said, you, you wanted to *investigate*...

GOULD: ...yes...

KAREN: ..."because once in a while"...

GOULD: ...yes.

KAREN: And once in a while one finds a pearl...

GOULD: Yes...

KAREN: And *this* book... I'm *telling* you, when you *read* it...

GOULD: Karen: it's about the end of the world.

KAREN: That's what I'm *saying*. That's why it...

GOULD: It's about the end of the world.

KAREN: Uh huh, uh huh. *(pause)* This book... *(pause)* This book... *(pause)* But you said someone's job was to read the manuscripts. *(pause)*

GOULD: Someone reads the manuscripts. Yes.

KAREN: ...that come in...

GOULD: ...yes. *(pause)* We have readers.

KAREN: Now: why do the readers read them?

GOULD: *(simultaneously with "read")* I get it. I get it. Yes. As I said. Yes. Once in a while, in a great while, yes, that...

KAREN: Why not this? I'm telling you...

GOULD: Look: I'm going to pay you the compliment of being frank. *(pause)* I'm going to talk to you. *(pause)* *Power*, people who are given a slight power, tend to think, they think that they're the only one that has these ideas, pure ideas, whatever, no matter. And, listen to me. Listen. I'm going to tell you. This book. Your book. On the end of the world which has meant so much to you, as I see that it has: won't make a good movie. Okay? I could tell you many things to influence you. But why? I have to respect your enthusiasm. And I *do* respect it. But this book, you want us to make, won't get the asses in the seats. Sounds crass? Whatever the thing just may be. My job: my job, my new job...is not even to "make," it is to "suggest," to "push," to champion...good work, I hope...choosing *from* those things which the public will come in to see. If they don't come to see it, what's the point? You understand? *(pause)* This is what I do. You said a certain kind of courage to embrace a fact? *(pause)* This is the

94

fact here.

KAREN: Why do you... *(pause)* Your job is to make movies people will come see.

GOULD: That's right.

KAREN: Why do you think they won't come see this one? *(pause)* Are you ever wrong? Do you see what I'm asking? Just because you think it is "too good"...I...I...I think they would come see it. *(pause)* *I* would. It's about...it's about what we feel. *(pause)*

GOULD: It is?

KAREN: Yes.

GOULD: Which is...

KAREN: Everyone is frightened.

GOULD: Everyone is frightened.

KAREN: Everything is breaking down.

GOULD: It is?

KAREN: Yes.

GOULD: It is?

KAREN: Yes. It's over...

GOULD: It...

KAREN: I believe it is.

GOULD: ...the...

KAREN: ...things as we know them.

GOULD: Are over?

KAREN: Of course they are. Do you see? We don't have to *deny* it... The *power* that this thought will release...in, in, in *everyone*. Something which speaks to them...this book spoke to *me*. It changed me...I...

GOULD: Yes, but quite frankly the fact that it changed *you*, that *you* like it, that you'd like to see it "go" is not sufficient reason for the studio to pay fifteen million dollars to put it up there.

KAREN: A sufficient reason.

GOULD: Yes.

KAREN: To make the film.

GOULD: Yes. *(pause)*

KAREN: Someone, someone makes a decision to, someone can make a decision to...

GOULD: Richard Ross.

KAREN: You're going to see him tomorrow, you could...look. Look, I *read* the script. Mister Fox's script, the prison film. That's, that's *degradation*, that's the same old...it's despicable, it's... It's degrading to the human spirit...it...

GOULD: It *what*...?

KAREN: Of course; this rage...it's killing people, meaningless...the sex, the titillation, violence...people don't want, they don't *want*, they...they don't want this.

GOULD: Of course they do, that's what we're in business to *do*, don't you underst...that's what we're in business to do. *Make the thing everyone made last year. Make that image people want to see.* That *is* what they, it's more than what they want. It is what they require. And it's my job. That's my job...when I tell Ross about the Douglas Brown film, he's going to fall upon my neck and *kiss* me. *You* know that. *You* know that I can't make this book.

KAREN: I *don't* know that.

GOULD: I *told* you...

KAREN: You held out a hope to me, this morning...

GOULD: ...I help out a hope...

KAREN: ...that's what I said...

GOULD: Aha! You see? That's what *you* said... We all, as I said, everyone has feelings, *everyone* would like to "make a difference." Everyone says "I'm a maverick" but we're, *you* know that, just one part of the whole, nobody's a maverick.

KAREN: But...

GOULD: Now: what I told you was: it was a "courtesy read."

KAREN: ...I, I don't like to be naive...

GOULD: ...I told you what the chances were...

KAREN: ...I don't think it's attractive, and I don't think it's right. To be naive. But...

GOULD: I *told* you what the deal was. Don't you understand?

KAREN: But I...

GOULD: But *you*. Yes. Everyone is trying to "promote" me...

Don't you *know* that? Don't you *care*? Don't you *care*? *Every move I make*, do you understand? Everyone *wants* something from me.

KAREN: *(pause)* Yes. I understand that.

GOULD: You understand that?

KAREN: Yes, I do.

GOULD: Well, if you understand that, then *how can you act this way?*

KAREN: To come here...

GOULD: Yes.

KAREN: ...you asked me here. *(pause)* I knew what the deal was. I know you wanted to sleep with me. You're right, I came anyway; you're right.

GOULD: ...To sleep with you...

KAREN: Didn't you?

GOULD: No...

KAREN: Why lie? You don't have to lie.

GOULD: But you're wrong.

KAREN: But I'm *not* wrong. This is what I'm saying. Are we so poor...that we can't have those simple things: we want love, why should we deny it? Why should you? You could of asked me, you *did* ask me. I know what you meant. That's why I came.

GOULD: You came to...?

KAREN: I said why not? I'm weak, too. We all need companionship, the things we want... I wanted them. You're right. I shouldn't act as though I was naive. I shouldn't act as though I believed you. You're...but but but:

GOULD: I asked you here to sleep with me?

KAREN: Then I read the book. I, I, I've been depraved, too, I've been frightened, I know that you're frightened. I *know* what you are. You see. That's what I'm telling you.

GOULD: *I'm* frightened?

KAREN: I know that you are. I would have come here anyway. Is that depraved? *I* know what it is to be bad. I've been bad, I know what it is to be lost, I know you're lost. *I know* that... How we are afraid...to "ask," to even "ask," and say in jest, "Yes. I prayed to be pure"...but it was not an accident. That I came here. Sometimes it reaches for us. And we say "show me a sign." And when it reaches us, then we see we *are* the sign. And we find the answers. In the book...

GOULD: Why did you say you would come here anyway...

KAREN: ...listen to me: The Tramp said "Radiation." Well, *whatever* it had been, it makes no difference... Listen *(She reads.)* "What was coming was a return to the self, which is to say, a return to God. It was round. He saw all things were round. And the man saw that it all had been devoted to one end. That the diseases in the body were the same diseases in the world. That things were ending. *Yes.* That things *must* end. And that vouchsafed to him a vision of infinity"... You see?

GOULD: No.

KAREN: No?

GOULD: No, I don't understand.

KAREN: You don't understand.

GOULD: No.

KAREN: Would you like to understand? *(pause)* The things you've hoped for. The reasons you asked me here.

GOULD: I don't understand you.

KAREN: You wanted something—you were frightened.

GOULD: I was frightened?

KAREN: That forced you to lie. I forgive you.

GOULD: ...you forgive me...?

KAREN: You know how I can? Because we're just the same. You said you prayed to be pure.

GOULD: I said that...

KAREN: This morning.

GOULD: I was joking.

KAREN: I looked in your heart. I saw you. And people can need each other. That's what the book says. You understand? We needn't be afraid.

GOULD: I don't understand.

KAREN: You can if you wish to. In the world. Dying. We prayed for a sign. A temporary girl. You asked me to read the book. *(pause)* I read the book. Do you know what it says? It says that you were put here to make stories people need to see. To make them less afraid. It says in *spite* of our transgressions—that we could do something. Which would bring us alive. So that we needn't feel ashamed. *(pause)* We needn't feel frightened. The wild animal dies with pride. He didn't make the world. God made the world. You say that you prayed to be pure. What if your prayers were answered? You asked me to come. Here I am.

THE UNDOING
by William Mastrosimone
Poultry shop - Present - Lorraine (40's) - Berk (30-40)

Lorraine - A bitter, alcholic proprietor of a poultry shop
Berk - A wounded man in Lorraine's employ

Lorraine is a hard-drinking woman haunted by her husband's
death at the hands of a drunk driver. Berk is a man who simply
appears at her poultry shop one day. Lorraine gives him a job
in the killing room. Unknown to Lorraine, Berk is the man
responsible for her husband's death. Here, the guilt-ridden Berk
does his best to persuade Lorraine to get sober.

LORRAINE: Berk!
BERK: *(Offstage)* Yeah?
LORRAINE: Inside.
BERK: *(Entering)* Yeah?
LORRAINE: I don't need you.
BERK: What?
LORRAINE: You're fired.
BERK: I do something wrong?
LORRAINE: I need sex.
BERK: What's that?
LORRAINE: You don't want to work here. It don't get better.
BERK: You don't know who I am.
LORRAINE: Another cripple who can't do anything else. Who else
would do this work?
BERK: Look at me. You know who I am?
LORRAINE: I know you, I attract freaks. I go through one every two
or three weeks. In three days I'd have you drinking again. Get out.
(He starts to hand up his apron.) How? How? How'd you get off the
juice and not lose your fuckin' mind?
BERK: You got to want to come up again.
LORRAINE: Want to? Suppose you don't want to? Answer me that.
How do you want to if you don't want to? No answer for that, right
or wrong, one-eye?

100

THE UNDOING

BERK: You didn't hit bottom yet.

LORRAINE: What bottom? There's no bottom. It goes and it goes and it goes and you keep falling and nothing stops you, nothing, and I fall when I lay in my bed and think I'm dying and I don't care. I don't care until I think of Mosca and Corvo running to see the cops come and force my door and carry my corpse out under the sheet, and they come in and look to see how I lived and they talk, all their talk. So don't talk this life-is-beautiful bullshit until you tell me how to care if you don't care.

BERK: I don't know.

LORRAINE: You're goddamn right you don't know, because it can't happen. Hit the bricks, Mister. Go on. Go on. Wait. I'll write a check.

BERK: Don't worry about it.

LORRAINE: How many hours you work?

BERK: Five minutes.

LORRAINE: I'll pay you for two hours.

BERK: Forget it.

LORRAINE: You stay right here, Mister, and you take this check. *(She dashes off the check so quickly that we know it can't be legible. She hands it go BERK. He rips it up and drops the pieces in the barrel.)* Who says there's a bottom?

BERK: I say.

LORRAINE: You been there?

BERK: Yeah.

LORRAINE: How do you know you hit bottom?

BERK: You feel like you got to die to get better. You been there?

LORRAINE: I live there? *(Pause)* Grab a bird.

BERK: What?

LORRAINE: You want to work here or not?

BERK: Sure.

LORRAINE: Don't go. Please, don't go. What's the matter?

BERK: I don't like that noise.

LORRAINE: The first one's hard.

BERK: Does it get easier?

101

THE UNDOING

LORRAINE: After a while it's like driving a car.

BERK: What do you mean?

LORRAINE: You don't even think about it.

LORRAINE: He was a selfish lying heartless sonofagaddamnbitchin-bastard. But I was Pazz *(From "Pazzo", crazy, pronounced "Pots")* for him.

BERK: What's that?

LORRAINE: Pazz, pazz. —Don't you speak English?

BERK: I thought I did.

LORRAINE: Pazz is when you know you shouldn't do something but you do it anyway because you can't help it. *(Pause)* How can you live on seventy-five a week?

BERK: I don't need much, anymore.

LORRAINE: I'll make it one twenty-five, and double it when you learn.

BERK: Don't worry about it.

LORRAINE: I don't want to lose you.

BERK: You won't.

LORRAINE: I got a room upstairs.

BERK: To rent?

LORRAINE: Furnished.

BERK: Yeah?

LORRAINE: The guy before had it.

BERK: What happened to him?

LORRAINE: He quit on me.

BERK: What's it go for?

LORRAINE: It's yours. Watch out around here. Walls are thin. You sneeze and the lady down the street says God-bless.

BERK: How much?

LORRAINE: Don't worry about it.

BERK: No, how much?

LORRAINE: Don't worry about it.

BERK: Bed?

LORRAINE: Rollaway.

BERK: Stove?

THE UNDOING

LORRAINE: You got to hook it up.

BERK: Fridge?

LORRAINE: Small.

BERK: Perfect.

LORRAINE: I can give you linens and things.

BERK: I appreciate it.

LORRAINE: Sure.

BERK: How much?

LORRAINE: Don't worry about it.

BERK: Thanks.

LORRAINE: You can take the fan up there.

BERK: Don't need it.

LORRAINE: It's an oven up there. —Coffee?

BERK: Thanks.

(She pours two cups. LORRAINE pours liquor in hers, starts to put the cap on, pauses, pours some liquor in his coffee, puts the bottle away.)

LORRAINE: Feel the vein?

BERK: Yeah.

LORRAINE: Do it. *(Pause)* What's the matter?

BERK: It hangs there so still.

LORRAINE: It knows it's time.

BERK: Think so?

LORRAINE: Make it clean. The way the priest wipes the chalice clean after he eats the wafer and drinks the wine. One, two, three. Clean.

BERK: I see.

LORRAINE: What would make me want to come up?

BERK: To feel again.

LORRAINE: Feel what?

BERK: A hand. A mouth. A dog's head. A baby. Hear Sinatra. Or rain on the roof. Laugh. Taste good food. Feel.

LORRAINE: If I felt again, they'd have to tie me down and gag me.

(She sips her coffee. He sips his, pause, spits it out on the floor.)

BERK: What's this?

LORRAINE: JD.

(Pause)
BERK: Why'd you do this?
LORRAINE: So I could watch.
BERK: Watch what?
LORRAINE: You.
BERK: Do what?
LORRAINE: To see if you still want it.
BERK: I don't.
LORRAINE: Bullshit.
BERK: I don't.
LORRAINE: You sneak it, right or wrong?
BERK: Not a drop.
LORRAINE: You're a liar.
BERK: You don't believe me because you're too weak to quit.
LORRAINE: You can't just chuck the juice! You drank until you landed in the hospital and they took it away from you.
BERK: The guys brought me stuff. I poured it down the sink.
LORRAINE: Take a drink and show me you don't need another one.
(He takes the cup and puts it to his lips. They share a long hard look.)
Prove it to me!
BERK: Nobody can prove nothin' to you. *(He dumps it out.)*
LORRAINE: You phony! You sneak it.
BERK: Think what you want.
LORRAINE: You're a sneak. Show me! Show me! *(She offers the bottle.)*
BERK: No thanks.
LORRAINE: Nobody just chucks the juice!
BERK: You're so dead inside, you want everybody else around you to be dead.
LORRAINE: If you was me you'd drown yourself in it.
BERK: I was worse than you. Much worse.
LORRAINE: Nothin's worse than me! I drink not to feel! Not to see! Not to hear!
(A siren passes. She takes a deep drink from the bottle.)
BERK: And a dog has to eat its own vomit.

THE UNDOING

(As if the liquor has turned to vomit in her mouth, she spits it out.)
LORRAINE: A siren goes by and I have to live it all again. Two, three, four times a day. Three, four, five times a night. *(Addressing the siren)* How many times can I live it again! *(The siren kindly goes away. Pause.)* I'm in bed. Waiting for Leo to come home. I hear a knock. Mosca and Corva. 'Come quick.' 'What's amatter?' 'Leo.' They pull me and Lorr down the street. Sirens and flashers, red and blue, red and blue, spinning faster than my head. Cop cars and fire engine headlights aimed at two car wrecks stuck together. Cops with crowbars tearing at the doors. Firemen with chain saws. Paramedics on the hood of the car that ran the STOP sign, pull the man out the windshield. He's dead. They stretch him out and wire his chest and electrify his heart and give him life again. And in the other car, a screaming man with a broken steering wheel in his chest and blood on his face, calls my name...'Lorraine'...'Lorraine'...and it's Leo's voice. And I see him. And he sees me. And I laugh. That's right. A laugh as big as a car wreck. It just pukes out of me, all the years and all the talk and all the cups of coffee and the fights and the making-up and the nights he flicked his headlights in the alley and I'd climb out my window when I was fifteen and he was thirty-one and we'd skinnydip in the quarry and he'd throw a blanket on the roof of his '57 Chevy and turn up the radio and he'd laugh and love me and bite me and adore me and destroy me with his pleasure till the birds sang and hold me like he wanted to break me in half...and I laugh. Out in the street. And he was nothing to me. Just another chicken in the barrel flapping around. Nothing. I laugh and the cops stop. The firemen, the paramedics stop. Police dogs stop. The air, the world, the moon, stop. *(She drinks. He takes the bottle.)* Give me that. *(He tosses it in the killing room. It shatters.)* You one-eye cripple! *(She finds another bottle. They contend for it. He wins.)*
LORRAINE: *Get out!*
(He grabs her arm, takes the bottle, tosses it away. She breaks, he holds her.)
LORRAINE: Make me feel again... *(He lifts her. The lights fade and the phone rings.)* Up there... Up, up, up there... Make me pazz again...up.

WHEN WE WERE WOMEN
by Sharman Macdonald
Scotland during WWII - Isla (20's) - MacKenzie (20-30)

Isla - A young woman
MacKenzie - A Chief Petty Officer in the Royal Navy

Isla and MacKenzie are both caught out of doors during an air
raid. When they encounter one another on a darkened country
road there is an immediate attraction betweem them.

*(ISLA is sitting by a lamp post. MACKENZIE crawls across the road
to her.)*
MACKENZIE: What the hell.
ISLA: I can't see in the dark.
MACKENZIE: What are you doing out?
ISLA: My torch is broken.
MACKENZIE: There's bombs falling from the sky.
ISLA: I've bumped my head.
(The all-clear sounds. MACKENZIE salutes the heavens.)
MACKENZIE: Here. Give it here.
ISLA: What.
MACKENZIE: Give me the torch.
ISLA: I walked into the lamp post.
MACKENZIE: That was smart.
ISLA: You're not very sympathetic. My head's sore. *(MACKENZIE
shakes the torch.)* My face is all wet. *(The beam comes on.)* Am I
bleeding. *(MACKENZIE takes out a handkerchief and wipes her face.)*
Is that clean? *(MACKENZIE looks at her.)* Well?
MACKENZIE: You've a cut over your eye.
ISLA: Do I look awful?
MACKENZIE: What were you out for?
ISLA: None of your business.
MACKENZIE: Manners. Manners.
ISLA: Ow.
MACKENZIE: Sorry.
ISLA: I'm alright.

WHEN WE WERE WOMEN

MACKENZIE: What was so important?

ISLA: I had a bet on.

MACKENIZIE: You'll need stitches in that.

ISLA: No one's stitching me. I know you.

MACKENZIE: My God. My God. Covered in blood. It's the Spanish Princess.

ISLA: Eh?

MACKENZIE: I know you.

ISLA: Say that again.

MACKENZIE: What?

ISLA: That. What you called me.

MACKENZIE: Spanish Princess.

ISLA: That's nice.

MACKENZIE: You. You water the beans in that canteen.

ISLA: I do not.

MACKENZIE: Aye you do.

ISLA: I don't.

MACKENZIE: Think you can stand?

ISLA: I can stand.

MACKENZIE: Here. *(He holds out his hand. She doesn't take it.)*

ISLA: I'm fine.

MACKENZIE: Are you now?

ISLA: I do not water the beans.

MACKENZIE: Where's your hat?

ISLA: I haven't got one.

MACKENZIE: You canny be a lady if you havenie got a hat. *(Someone lifts the blackout blind behind them. A shaft of light streams out. A voice shouts, 'Aileen'. The light goes out. A figure stands at an open window. MACKENZIE grabs ISLA's elbow. He takes her into the shadow.)* No that I'm that fond of ladies mind.

ISLA: Are you not.

MACKENZIE: That's no where my heart lies.

(ISLA shakes free of him. She tries to walk away. She stumbles. He steadies her.)

ISLA: I'm alright.

MACKENZIE: I'll see you home.

ISLA: You will not.

MACKENZIE: My old Gran said always to take care of damsels in distress.

ISLA: My Gran said 'Keep your haund on your Ha'penny.'

MACKENZIE: Is that right?

ISLA: I know you. You with your raincoat. You think you're God's gift you do. The lot of you. Don't think I don't know you.

MACKENZIE: Here.

(He gives her the torch. She walks away. The torch goes out.)

ISLA: Oh. Oh damn. *(Takes another couple of steps.)* It's no me. The beans. They come like that. The beans. *(Shakes the torch. It doesn't come on.)* I can't see in the dark. *(Shakes the torch. It doesn't come on.)* Please.

MACKENZIE: What was the bet.

ISLA: I'm not telling you.

MACKENZIE: Night. Night.

ISLA: Come here.

MACKENZIE: Well?

ISLA: I want you to take me...

MACKENZIE: Night. Night.

ISLA: Please.

MACKENZIE: The bet.

ISLA: Half a pint of gin.

MACKENZIE: Eh?

ISLA: Straight down.

MACKENZIE: Down what. Down where.

ISLA: Well it wouldnie be down the stank would it?

MACKENZIE: You were gonnie drink a half-pint of gin.

ISLA: So what?

MACKENZIE: A whole half-pint.

ISLA: Down in one an' stay standin' up.

MACKENZIE: I'll see you home.

ISLA: I don't want to go home.

MACKENZIE: Home.

WHEN WE WERE WOMEN

ISLA: No.

MACKENZIE: What are you? Are you daft? I mean I like alcohol. I'm no sayin' I don't like alcohol. Home.

ISLA: I'm a grown woman.

MACKENZIE: Are you now?

ISLA: I can do what I like.

MACKENZIE: You treat alcohol wi' respect. Look at you. You canny stand up right. I'll get you to your own home if I have to carry you there. And don't you think I can't. I've carried heavier than you. *(He holds out his arm.)*

ISLA: I think I'd be safer wi' the gin.

MACKENZIE: I'll tell you something.

ISLA: What?

MACKENZIE: Right at this very moment you're no that appealing. I mean, when yer cleaned up a bit you might just pass muster. But right now, right now... *(She takes his arm. They walk.)* Spanish Princess. For your hair an' your hips an' your dark, dark eyes and the way you look at me and your hands wi' their great long fingers an' their red, red nails an' your shoulders an' your shoes an' your white, white socks. See they socks God. Women in white socks God. My God. We're all poor sinners in this vale of tears.

THE YOUNG LADY FROM TACNA
by Mario Vargas Llosa
translated by David Graham-Young
Peru - 1950's - Mamae (20's) - Joaquín (20's)

Mamae - A young woman being courted
Joaquín - Mamae's devoted suitor

Mamae, a dying old woman, becomes tranformed into her younger self as she remembers her handsome young suitor, Joaquín, and the time he visited her shortly before they were to be married.

JOAQUIN: *(Whispering, as if leaning over a wrought-iron grille or balcony)* Elvira...Elvira...Elvira... *(MAMAE opens her eyes. She listens; smiles mischievously and looks around; she is flustered and excited. Her movements and speech are now those of a young woman.)*
MAMAE: Joaquín! But he's out of his mind. At this hour! Uncle and Aunt are going to hear him.
JOAQUIN: I know you're there, I know you can hear me. Come out, just for a second, Elvira. I've got something important to say to you. You know what it is, don't you? You're beautiful, I love you, and I want you. I can hardly wait till Sunday—I'm literally counting the hours.
(MAMAE sits up. Although clearly delighted, she remains demure and reticent. She goes over to the wrought-iron grille.)
MAMAE: Whatever do you mean by coming here at this hour, Joaquín? Didn't anyone see you? You're going to ruin my reputation. Here in Tacna the walls have ears.
JOAQUIN: *(voraciously kissing MAMAE's hands)* I was already in bed, my love. When suddenly I had this feeling, right here in my breast; it was like an order from a general, which I had to obey: 'If you hurry, you'll find her still awake,' it seemed to say. 'Make haste, fly to her house.' It's true, Elvira. I had to see you. And touch you.
(He eagerly tries to grasp her round the waist, but she shies away from him.) If I hadn't been able to see you, I wouldn't have slept a wink all night...

110

MAMAE: But we spent all afternoon together, Joaquín! What a lovely walk we had in the garden with my cousin! When I heard you, I was just thinking about all those pomegranates and pear trees, quinces and peaches. And the river, wasn't it looking lovely too? How I'd like to go plunging into the Caplina again sometime, just as I used to when I was a little girl.

JOAQUIN: This summer, if we're still in Tacna, I'll take you to the Caplina. We'll go at night. When no one will see us. To that same pool we had tea at this afternoon. We'll take off all our clothes...

MAMAE: Oh hush, Joaquín, don't start...!

JOAQUIN: ...and bathe together naked. We'll play in the water. I'll chase you and when I catch you...

MAMAE: Please, Joaquín! Don't be so uncouth.

JOAQUIN: But we're getting married on Sunday.

MAMAE: I won't have you being discourteous to me when I'm your wife either.

JOAQUIN: But I respect you more than anything in the world, Elvira. I even respect you more than my uniform. And you know what a uniform means to a soldier, don't you? Look, I couldn't be discourteous to you, even if I wanted to. I'm making you annoyed, I know. I do it deliberately. Because I like it when you're like this.

MAMAE; When I'm like what?

JOAQUIN: You're such a sensitive little flower. Everything seems to shock you, you're so easily intimidated, and you blush at the least provocation.

MAMAE: Isn't that how well-brought-up young women should behave?

JOAQUIN: Of course it is, Elvira, my love. You can't imagine how I ache for Sunday. The thought of having you all to myself, without any chaperons. To know that you depend on me for the slightest thing. What fun I'm going to have with you when we're alone together: I'll sit you on my knee and make you scratch me in the dark like a little kitten. Oh, and I'll win that bet. I'll count every hair on your head; there'll be more then five thousand, you'll see.

MAMAE: Are you going to count them on our wedding night?

THE YOUNG LADY FROM TACNA

JOAQUIN: Not on our wedding night, no. Do you want to know what I'm going to do to you on our wedding night?

MAMAE: *(Covering her ears)* No! No, I don't! *(They laugh. MAMAE mellows.)* Will you be as loving and affectionate as this after we're married, I wonder? You know what Carmencita said to me on our way back from the walk: 'You've really come up trumps with Joaquín, you know. He's good-looking, well-mannered, in fact quite the little gentleman in every way.'

JOAQUIN: Is that what you think too? You mean you don't mind that I'm a Chilean any more? And you've got used to the idea of being one yourself?

MAMAE: No, I have not. I'm a Peruvian, and that's the way I'm going to stay. I'll never forgive those loathsome bullies who won the war. Not till the day I die.

JOAQUIN: It's going to be very funny, you know. I mean, when you're my wife, and I'm posted to the garrison in Santiago or Antofagasta, are you going to spend all day arguing with my fellow officers about the War of the Pacific? Because if you say things like that about the Chileans, you'll get me court-martialled for high treason.

MAMAE: I'd never jeopardize your career, Joaquín. Whatever I think of the Chileans, I'll keep it strictly to myself. I'll smile and make eyes at your fellow officers.

JOAQUIN: That's enough of that! There'll be no smiling or making eyes at anybody. Don't you know I'm as jealous as a Turk? Well, with you, I'm going to be even worse.

MAMAE: You must go now. If my aunt and uncle found you here, they'd be so upset.

JOAQUIN: Your aunt and uncle. They've been the bane of our engagement.

MAMAE: Don't say that, not even in fun. Where would I be now if it hadn't been for Uncle Menelao and Aunt Amelia? I'd have been put in the orphanage in Tarapacá Street. Yes, along with all the bats.

JOAQUIN: I know how good they've been to you. And I'm glad they brought you up like some rare exotic bird. But we have been engaged for a whole year now and I've hardly been alone with you once! All

112

right, I know, you're getting anxious. I'm on my way.

MAMAE: Till tomorrow then, Joaquín. At the eight o'clock Mass in the Cathedral, same as usual?

JOAQUIN: Yes, same as usual. Oh, I was forgetting. Here's that book you lent me. I tried to read Federico Barreto's poems, but I couldn't keep my eyes open. You read them for me, when you're tucked up snug in your little bed.

MAMAE: *(Pulling out a hair from her head and offering it to him)* I'll whisper them in your ear one day—then you'll like them. I'm glad I'm marrying you, Joaquín.

(Before he leaves, JOAQUIN tries to kiss her on the mouth, but she turns her face away and offers him her cheek. As she goes back towards her armchair, she gradually takes on the characteristics of an old woman again.)

ZORA NEALE HURSTON
by Laurence Holder
New York City - 1920's-40's - Zora - Herbert

Zora Neale Hurston - A visionary black American writer
Herbert Sheen - Zora's fiance

Zora Neale Hurston was an outspoken and ground-breaking
writer/anthropologist who devoted her creative talents to
portraying American Blacks in an accurate and non-patronizing
manner. This zeal produced such classics as "Mule-Bone."
Here, her fiance, Herbert, expects the Bohemian Zora to be a
traditional wife and mother.

HERBERT: What are you doing now, Zora?

ZORA: Herbert?

HERBERT: I asked you what you were doing sitting here on this bench
smoking. You know that's no way for a woman to be acting.

ZORA: I'm uppity, Herbert.

HERBERT: Yes, but the woman who is going to be my wife can't be
acting like that. There is a proper way to behave and you know it.

ZORA: Herbert, you are sounding like America, you know.

HERBERT: Just what's that mean?

ZORA: It means, Herbert, that even though you and I are engaged,
you are engaged to *me*.

HERBERT: I'm here to collect you and take you back home where you
can act like a woman is supposed to act.

ZORA: And just how is that?

HERBERT: I work and bring home the bacon. You keep the house
clean, the pots rattling, and the children happy. That's what marriage
is to me and I thought it meant the same to you.

ZORA: Marriage can mean that, but maybe I should warn you, it
never meant that to me.

HERBERT: Zora, I wish you would stop talking like that. I'm a man
and you're a woman.

ZORA: You take my breath away, Herbert.

HERBERT: I'm here to collect you, girl.

ZORA NEALE HURSTON

ZORA: Herbert, are you sure you want to jump over the broom with me, though?

HERBERT: Of course I'm sure. I wouldn't be here if I wasn't sure.

ZORA: I've seen and done things you might not approve of.

HERBERT: You want to be more specific, girl.

ZORA: No. But maybe you should stop and think some more about it. I mean, it pleases a woman to be wanted, Herbert. I just don't know if I can do all those things you think a woman is supposed to do. Herbert, I am an artist, an anthropologist, a writer. I'm writing a play with the famous Langston Hughes.

HERBERT: Langston who?

ZORA: You don't know who Langston Hughes is?

HERBERT: I don't know the man, but if he isn't going to marry you, then he's worthless.

ZORA: Oh, Herbert, you say all the right things, but won't you please look at me and see that I have changed? I'm going to give you a hard time.

HERBERT: That's what wives are supposed to do. Keep men in line.

ZORA: I see. That's what you want from me—to keep you in line.

HERBERT: I want you to fix my eggs in the morning.

ZORA: Herbert, I am not going to stay in bed and fix your eggs every morning.

HERBERT: That doesn't matter.

ZORA: It doesn't matter? Well, then, I'm not going to have six kids by you, either.

HERBERT: But that's romantic, Zora.

ZORA: It may be romantic, Herbert—just you and me and all those crumb snatchers in your mind—but it just isn't me. Herbie, please.

HERBERT: Zora, I don't care. It doesn't matter. You're the only one who does. And my family is just dying to see you.

ZORA: I know they're not dying to see me with my bohemian self slapped all over their couches, smoking ragweed or whatever else comes along. That's not what they have in mind for you, Herbie.

HERBERT: I don't care what they have in mind, Zora.

ZORA: Boy, if you don't care, if you are sure you don't care, then I don't care. I'm just flattered.

SECTION II

Two Women

BACK STREET MAMMY
by Trish Cooke
London - Present - Dynette (16) - Jackie (16)

Dynette - A young woman faced with an unwanted pregnancy
Jackie - Dynette's best friend

The daughter of West Indian immigrants, Dynette fears that she
is pregnant. Here, she and her best friend discuss the moral
implications of an abortion.

(DYNETTE is washing her face.)
JACKIE: Hey Dynette.
DYNETTE: Hi Jack was I missed yesterday?
JACKIE: I signed your name in the late book. As long as no one
checks up you're clear. Where did you go?
DYNETTE: To see our Jan.
JACKIE: She all right? How's the little one? Sorry. I mean your
niece...Tania...sorry.
DYNETTE: Why you sorry?
JACKIE: Didn't mean to remind you...
DYNETTE: Don't be daft.
JACKIE: What's the latest anyway?
DYNETTE: Latest?
JACKIE: Any sign of the Dreaded Curse?
(JACKIE puts her fingers up as a Dracula Shield.)
DYNETTE: No.
JACKIE: What about the exams?
(DYNETTE looks at her. JACKIE shuts up. Pause.)
DYNETTE: I might have an abortion.
JACKIE: You wouldn't...
DYNETTE Wouldn't I? I'm scared Jack.
JACKIE: Does your Mum know?
DYNETTE: No. I swear you say anything and I'll kill you.
JACKIE: I wouldn't.
DYNETTE: I've never thought about abortion before. Never thought
about what it means.

116

BACK STREET MAMMY

JACKIE: It means to terminate the...

DYNETTE: I know that, stupid cow, I know what it means in the dictionary but to me it means I'm going to lose my God.

(JACKIE looks puzzled.) Everything I've been taught to respect. The unquestionable. God's laws. I'm challenging God's laws Jackie. What does that make me...? 'Thou shalt not kill'. I just want another chance. And for the first time in my life it feels like what I say, what I decide counts. And funny thing is I know God's not going to punish me. Nobody's going to strike me down...

JACKIE: You need to talk to somebody.

DYNETTE: But I do. *She* doesn't answer me back or tell me what to do. She listens. She just lies comfortably inside me. *(She laughs.)* She is me Jackie. I found a new God. My own.

JACKIE: Stop it Dynette you're messing about. *(She makes the sign of the cross.)* She doesn't mean it God. For Christ's sake, you've only just missed a period. There's nothing there. You're not pregnant!

DYNETTE: I'm changing.

JACKIE: You're telling me!

DYNETTE: You can't understand. Nobody can, not even our Jan because Tania is Tania but this is something that's me, that thinks me and breathes me.

JACKIE: Breathes you?

DYNETTE: I'm discovering things about myself that I didn't know before. I'm finding out what I want and when I go to bed we talk.

JACKIE: Who?

DYNETTE: Me and my God. I ask her if she'd mind if I postponed her birth...

JACKIE *(curiously)*: And what does she say?

DYNETTE: She listens...she just wraps herself around me and makes me know that whatever I decide is right. I'd like to hold her. I dream of her knees locked round my waist and her arms tight around my shoulders...and her head on my chest. She's not a baby. She's my friend and it feels warm when we're like that...safe...love. I've never been so close to anyone before in my life.

JACKIE: So...what you going to do...*if* you are...?

DYNETTE: What d'you think about abortion Jack?

JACKIE: It's murder.

DYNETTE: I can't have a baby. Look at me. What would I do with a baby! There's so much I've got to do first. I don't want to end up like Mum.

JACKIE: You're not pregnant, you're not. You can't be...it's the pill it sometimes messes up your system.

DYNETTE: I never went on the pill.

JACKIE: But we talked... I know you never went with me but I thought...

DYNETTE: It was too late.

(Pause.)

JACKIE: Me and Terry finished last night.

DYNETTE: Oh.

JACKIE: He said I'm a teaser, I told him I wasn't ready.

(JACKIE leaves.)

DYNETTE: I'm not ready.

THE CEMETERY CLUB
by Ivan Menchell
Queens - Present - Ida (50-60) - Lucille (50-60)

Ida - A widow
Lucille - A widow

Ida and Lucille are two widows who, along with their friend,
Doris, make regular visits to their husbands' graves. On one
such occasion, Ida and Lucille take a moment to chat while
waiting for Doris to arrive.

LUCILLE: Son of a bitch!

IDA: What's the matter?!

LUCILLE: A guy follows me all the way from Queens Boulevard,
undressing me with his eyes, and she asks what's the matter.

IDA: Again someone was following you?

LUCILLE: Can I help it if men find me attractive?

IDA: Who was it this time?

LUCILLE: I didn't get a name. He had blond hair, six one, six two,
about a hundred seventy pounds—a very nice build—with green eyes
and a cleft chin—

IDA: What were you, walking backwards?

LUCILLE: I happen to have an excellent memory... So what do you
think?

IDA: I think you should just forget the whole thing.

LUCILLE: I mean about the *coat*. Look at this how she doesn't even
notice.

IDA: Oh Lucille, it's beautiful. New?

LUCILLE: Have you seen it on this gorgeous body before?

IDA: You should wear it in the best of health.

LUCILLE: You ready for the best part? Guess how much.

IDA: A coat like that you must have paid at least three thousand.

LUCILLE: Nope.

IDA: Less?

LUCILLE: Much.

IDA: What, twenty-five hundred?

THE CEMETERY CLUB

(LUCILLE joyously shakes her head.)

IDA: Don't tell me it was under two thousand.

LUCILLE: *Nineteen fifty.*

IDA: I'm fainting.

LUCILLE: Is that a steal or is that a steal?

IDA: Where did you find it?

LUCILLE: Well, I was walking in Manhattan down Fifty-seventh Street when I pass the Ritz Thrift Shop. Usually, I would never even look in the window. I mean, what could they have - garbage, right? This time I happen to look and what do you think I see?

IDA: That coat.

LUCILLE: No. I see a full length brown fox you could die from. I go in, try it on and my mazel it's a little too tigh— *(She's about to say "tight" but stops herself.)* —short. Then as I'm walking out, I'm looking down the rack and what do you think catches my eye?

IDA: That coat.

LUCILLE: A leopard jacket that made my heart stop. But for how often I'd get to wear it, it didn't pay.

IDA: Lucille, we're not getting younger. Where did you find the mink?

LUCILLE: So, as I'm about to leave I see them bringing in a new rack and what do you think is the first thing I spot?

IDA: Who knows?

LUCILLE: This coat.

IDA: Thank God.

LUCILLE: There's only one thing that bothers me.

IDA: What?

LUCILLE: Knowing it was someone else's. I mean, who knows who this person is? All I know is that she's tall, terrifically slim and probably didn't look half as good in it as I do.

IDA: So what are you worried? You got a gorgeous coat at a great price.

LUCILLE: Ida, why would she give this coat up?

IDA: Who knows? Maybe she died.

LUCILLE: Oh my God. I didn't even think. This poor woman could be dead. For all I know, she could have died in this coat. The poor thing could've been wearing this coat, crossing the street and got hit by a car. It's not marked anywhere, it it? *(SHE turns around to show Ida the back of the coat.)*

IDA: It's perfect. Not a scratch on it...except for that one tire mark down the back.

LUCILLE; Oh!

IDA: I'm only kidding. There's nothing on it. Let me try it on.

LUCILLE: My pleasure.

(LUCILLE takes off the coat and gives it to Ida. SHE puts it on.)

IDA: How do I look?

LUCILLE: Do the words "Lana Turner" mean anything?

IDA: Let me see.

(SHE runs over to the mirror and looks at herself. LUCILLE stands behind her.)

LUCILLE: What becomes a legend most!

IDA: *(Embarrassed.)* Oh...

LUCILLE: Maybe I'll take a look, see if they have another one. Picture the two of us out on the town, fur from head to toe.

IDA: It's not me.

LUCILLE: All the more reason.

IDA: I don't need it. *(SHE takes off the coat and hangs it up.)*

LUCILLE: Ida, no one buys a mink because they need it. You buy support hose because you need it. You buy a mink because you *want* it.

IDA: I don't want it. Besides, I couldn't afford it. Where did *you* get two thousand dollars?

LUCILLE: One of Harry's Municipals Bonds came due.

IDA: Well, congratulations. How about some tea?

LUCILE: Love it.

IDA: I'll put the water up.

(SHE exits to the kitchen. LUCILLE hangs the coat in the closet.)

LUCILLE: I want you to know I broke a pretty hot date to come here today.

IDA: *(Offstage.)* Who you got now?

THE CEMETERY CLUB

LUCILLE: His name's Donald, Ida, if I tell you.

IDA: Good looking?

LUCILLE: *Gorgeous... (Nonchalantly looking through Ida's mail.)* and a gentleman. Opens the door, pulls out the chair, picks up the check. We had a night Friday you wouldn't believe. Dinner, dancing, a hansom cab ride through Central Park.

IDA: *(Reenters.)* How romantic.

LUCILLE: And he didn't leave me alone all night. Hands everywhere.

IDA: No.

LUCILLE: Yeah.

IDA: So when do I meet him already?

LUCILLE: You'll meet him.

IDA: You never stay with one long enough for me to meet them.

LUCILLE: I'll tell you what—if we're still together next week I'll have him stop by during canasta. And what about you? When am I going to start hearing about a little romance, a little excitement?

IDA: When it happens you'll hear about it.

LUCILLE: I'm all ready to start double dating. I can't keep taking out two men by myself.

IDA: Why, they get tired?

(THEY laugh.)

LUCILLE: I'm serious, Ida. I'm waiting for you to join me. God knows Doris is never going to start.

IDA: I wonder where she is. It's after eleven. I figured she would've been here early. Today's an important day for her.

LUCILLE: It's always important to Doris. This is the high point of the month for her. She thinks about it for two weeks after and starts getting ready two weeks before. It's like a vicious cycle.

IDA: Sometimes a cycle is important. You know what to expect.

LUCILLE: Well, my cycle ended more years ago than I care to remember and that hasn't stopped me.

IDA: I just hope today goes well, I can't believe it's already her fourth anniversary.

LUCILLE: *Today's* her fourth anniversary? I completely forgot.

IDA: How could you?

LUCILLE: I can't keep up with the dates anymore.

IDA: You really should try.

LUCILLE: Sometimes I think we should stop this whole business altogether.

IDA: Lucille.

LUCILLE: I do.

IDA: ...I don't know myself anymore.

LUCILLE: You see.

IDA: So why do you keep coming?

LUCILLE: Don't think I haven't asked myself.

IDA: I'm serious.

LUCILLE: I like this time together.

(IDA smiles.)

LUCILLE: But I'm sure there's other ways we could spend the afternoon.

(The DOORBELL rings.)

IDA: *(Going to the door.)* Well don't bring it up today.

LUCILLE: I wouldn't say a word. Whatever she wants to talk, we'll talk.

IDA: You're a good friend.

LUCILLE: The best.

LA CHUNGA
by Mario Vargas Llosa
translated by David Graham-Young
Piura, Peru - 1945 - La Chunga (40-50) - Meche (20's)

La Chunga - A bar owner
Meche - A naive young prostitute

Meche has been brought to La Chunga's bar by her pimp. La Chunga desires the young woman and pays for her use for the evening. The two women retire to La Chunga's room, where the older woman warns Meche that her "boyfriend" will soon tire of her.

MECHE: *(With a nervous little laugh)* So now what happens? What's the game, Chunga?
(The cold woman of the previous scenes suddenly seems charged with life and sensuality.)
LA CHUNGA: It's not a game. I've paid three thousand sols for you. You're mine for the rest of the night.
MECHE: *(Defiantly)* Do you mean I'm your slave?
LA CHUNGA: For a few hours, at least. *(Handing her the glass)* Here. It'll calm your nerves.
(MECHE grasps the glass and takes a gulp.)
MECHE: Do you think I'm nervous? Well, you're wrong. I'm not afraid of you. I'm doing this for Josefino. If I wanted, I could push you aside and run out that door.
(LA CHUNGA sits on the bed.)
LA CHUNGA: But you won't. You said you'd obey me, and you're a woman of your word, I'm sure. Besides, you're just dying of curiosity, aren't you?
MECHE: *(Finishing the glass)* Do you honestly think you're going to get me drunk on two vermouths? Don't kid yourself. I've got a strong head for drink. I can go on all night without getting in the least bit tipsy. I can hold even more than Josefino.
(Pause.)
LA CHUNGA: Do to me what you do to him when you want to excite him.

LA CHUNGA

MECHE: *(With the same nervous little laugh)* I can't. You're a woman. You're Chunga.

LA CHUNGA: *(Coaxing and at the same time peremptory)* No. I am Josefino. Do to me what you do to him.

(Soft tropical music—boleros by Leo Marini or Los Panchos—can be heard in the distance. It conjures up images of couples dancing close, in a place full of smoke and alcohol. MECHE starts to undress, slowly, and rather awkwardly. Her voice seems forced, and unrelaxed.)

MECHE: You want to see me undress? Slowly, like this? This is how he likes it. Do you think I'm pretty? Do you like my legs? My breasts? I've got a nice firm body, look. No moles, no pimples, no flab. None of those things that make people so ugly. *(She has stripped down to her petticoat. She feels a little faint. She screws up her face.)* I can't, Chunga. You're not him. I can't believe what I'm doing or what I'm saying. I feel stupid, all this seems so unreal to me, so...

(She lets herself fall on the bed and stays there, face down, in a state of confusion; she is on the point of tears, but manages to restrain herself. LA CHUNGA gets up and sits beside her. She acts now with great sensitivity, as if moved by MECHE's discomfort.)

LA CHUNGA: The truth is, I admire you for being here. You surprised me, you know? I didn't think you would accept. *(Smoothes MECHE's hair.)* Do you love Josefino that much?

MECHE: *(Her voice a whisper)* Yes, I love him. *(Pause.)* But I don't think I did it just for him. But because of what you said too. I was curious. *(Turns to look at LA CHUNGA.)* You gave him three thousand *sols*. That's a lot of money.

LA CHUNGA: *(Passing her hand over MECHE's face, drying nonexistent tears.)* You're worth more than that. *(A hint of flirtatiousness becomes apparent through MECHE's resentment and embarrassment.)*

MECHE: Do you really like me, Chunga?

LA CHUNGA: You know very well I do. Or perhaps you didn't realize?

MECHE: Yes, I did. No other woman has ever looked at me like you did. You made me feel...so strange.

(LA CHUNGA puts hand round MECHE's shoulders and draws her to her. Kisses her. MECHE passively allows herself to be kissed. When

they separate MECHE gives a false little laugh.)
LA CHUNGA: You're laughing—so it can't have been that dreadful.
MECHE: How long have you been like this? I mean, have you always been...? Have you always liked women?
LA CHUNGA: I don't like *women*. I like you.
(She embraces her and kisses her. MECHE lets herself be kissed, but does not respond to LA CHUNGA's caresses. LA CHUNGA gently draws her face round and, still caressing her, orders her.) Open your mouth, slave. *(MECHE giggles nervously, and parts her lips. LA CHUNGA gives her a long kiss and this time MECHE raises her arm and puts it around LA CHUNGA's neck.)* That's it. I thought you didn't know how to kiss. *(Sarcastically)* Did you see little stars?
MECHE: *(Laughing)* Don't make fun of me.
LA CHUNGA: *(Holding her in her arms)* I'm not making fun of you. I want you to enjoy yourself tonight—more than you've ever enjoyed anything with that pimp.
MECHE: He's not a pimp! Don't say that word. He's in love with me. We may be getting married.
LA CHUNGA: He's a pimp. He sold you to me tonight. Next, he'll be taking you to the Casa Verde, to whore for him like all his other women. *(MECHE tries to slip away from her arms, pretending to be more angry than she really feels, but after a short struggle, she relents. LA CHUNGA puts her face close to hers and talks to her, almost kissing her.)* Let's not talk about that bum any more. Let's just talk about you and me.
MECHE: *(More calmly)* Don't hold me so tight, you're hurting.
LA CHUNGA: I can do what I want with you. You're my slave. *(MECHE laughs.)* Don't laugh. Repeat: I am your slave. *(Pause)*
MECHE: *(Laughs. Becoming serious)* It's only a game, isn't it? All right. I am your slave.
LA CHUNGA: I'm your slave and now I want to be your whore. *(Pause.)* Repeat.
MECHE: *(Almost in a whisper)* I'm your slave and now I want to be your whore.
(LA CHUNGA lays MECHE on the bed and starts to undress her.)
LA CHUNGA: So you will be.

126

EASTERN STANDARD
by Richard Greenberg
NYC restaurant - Present - Ellen (20's) - May (50-60)

Ellen - A waitress
May - A schizophrenic street person

Six people meet in a restaurant in New York City and become friends. Stephen, an architect who despises his job, falls in love with Phoebe, a Wall Street broker. Drew, Stephen's gay friend, is attracted to Phoebe's brother, Peter. Ellen and May are drawn into the group who gather at Stephen's summer home on Fire Island. Here, Ellen tries to expel May, who is drinking Perrier and screeching at the customers, from the restaurant.

(May is at the R. table. Her hair is snarled; her looks unhinged; her clothes ragtag and dirty. She nurses a Perrier. She mutters obscenities to herself, a low, steady litany.)
MAY: Fuckin' goddamn piss-ant shit, I'll kill him he gets a fuckin' son-of-a-bitch pisspot shitheel...[etc.] *(May notices Peter looking at her, looks at him fiercely.)* You lookin'a me? FUCK YOU! What? Am I CONSPICUOUS? You mother-fuckin' piece a— *(She notices someone at another table, D.L.)* And what are you lookin' at, lardass? What the *fuck* you think you're doin' here, huh, you look like a RHINOCEROS! Can't a woman just drink a Perrier in peace, GODDAMNIT! *(The waitress, Ellen, enters.)*
ELLEN: Excuse me?
MAY: *What?*
ELLEN: Would you please—?
MAY: *(Suddenly sweet.)* What, sweetheart?
ELLEN: Would you please lower you voice?
MAY: I don't know what you're talking about, sweetheart.
ELLEN: From its previous volume.
MAY: Sweet as a songbird.
ELLEN: Thank you.
MAY: *You mother-fuckin' cunt!*
ELLEN: I'm sorry, you're going to have to stop that or leave, you're

127

having a chaotic effect on lunch.

MAY: *(All of a sudden weepy.)* All I wanna do is sit here and drink my Perrier, nobody ever gives me a goddamn break, I just wanna sit here and I'm bein' heaped with this abuse, I don't—

ELLEN: I'm sorry, it's just that—

MAY: I gotta go out in the cold, I gotta fend for myself, I gotta—

ELLEN: *(Contrite.)* I know, I know, I'm sorry—

MAY: I got no future, no one to take care a me, you understan', don't you, sweetheart—

ELLEN: Of course, I'm—

MAY: *You revoltin' snatch.*

ELLEN: We have a five-dollar minimum.

MAY: ...*What?*

ELLEN: At lunch, a five-dollar minimum—

MAY: I can *pay*, you got no grounds for throwin' me out—

ELLEN: Actually, we do.

MAY: Yeah?

ELLEN: Your conversation; it's disturbing to the people around you.

MAY: My conversation is disturbin' to the people around me? *I'm* disturbin' *them*? Have you listened to *their* conversation?

ELLEN: I'm afraid—

MAY: Well, I suggest you do—

ELLEN: You'll—

MAY: —becasue it's all PRETTY INSIPID!

ELLEN: The manager would like you to leave.

MAY: Yeah? Well, why'n't he say so himself?

ELLEN: The manager, who is a chickenshit, would like you to leave and has delegated the responsibility for getting rid of you to me—

MAY: Honey, there's somethin' I gotta tell you—

ELLEN: Yes?

MAY: You're oppressed.

ELLEN: Thank you, I know.

MAY: We got that in common.

ELLEN: Yes, well—to tell the truth, I'd probably have a greater feeling of solidarity if you hadn't stolen my tip...

128

EASTERN STANDARD

MAY: Are you accusin' me of somethin'?

ELLEN: The guy who was sitting there before you? He comes every day, orders the same thing, leaves the same tip. Twenty-two percent.

MAY: Today he stiffed you, sweetheart.

ELLEN: He would not stiff me—

MAY: He stiffed you—

ELLEN: He would not stiff me because for months now he's been hoping to stiff me in another way, *capish*?

MAY: Fuckin' disgustin' men, my heart goes out to you, cookie.

ELLEN: *(A little gingerly.)* The manager would like you to leave.

MAY: Goddamn it, wherever I go it's the same thing—!

ELLEN: —I—

MAY: I'm on a grate, I'm in an alley, I'm in a hallway—train tracks, benches, vestibules, islands in the middle a' Broadway, I'm tryin' to sleep. I'm nursin' a cold, I'm tryin' to look like somethin' ya might possibly not wanna kill—somebody always comes along and says, "Move on." Well, where, where—where should I go? Tell me where to go and I'll go there. No, no, that's right, it's always, "Move on. Outta my sight. Wherever's not here." Trouble is, every place I get to's just another *here*. Well, I only got so much movin' in me. Somewhere along the line, somebody's gotta say, "Rest."

ELLEN: ...I'll be back.

MAY: Bless you, cookie... *(Ellen walks over to Peter and Phoebe, gives them menus.)* You miserable hooker... *(May guzzles Perrier. Ellen returns.)* So how are you, sweetheart-doll-angel?

ELLEN: Listen, I'm breaking every rule here.

MAY: Whattya talkin', sweetie?

ELLEN: Never fraternize with the customers—

MAY: Babydoll, I understan'—from my own waitressin' days—

ELLEN: You used to waitress?

MAY: What, you think I was *born* on the street? You think I spent my whole *life* in these clothes?

ELLEN: Well, I—

MAY: No *way*! I useta be lower middle class.

ELLEN: Uh-huh.

MAY: And you?

ELLEN: I'm an actress.

MAY: I figured.

ELLEN: Everybody does.

MAY: So what's your decision, honey?

ELLEN: ...What?

MAY: You're movin' toward, you're movin' away—

ELLEN: Oh, I—

MAY: So— Whaddya want—you wanna to hear my story?

ELLEN: Oh, I—

MAY: Uh-huh—

ELLEN: It's against the rules—I'm working now, I—

MAY: But it's what you want.

ELLEN: Let me take this table's order first. *(Peter has dropped his bombshell. Phoebe is stunned.)*

MAY: Go, sweetheart, go. *(Ellen goes to their table.)* You little bitch-in-heat. *(Ellen returns to May.)*

ELLEN: I'm back.

MAY: So, you wanna know about me?

ELLEN: Well... I've always been interested...

MAY: In me? I just got here.

ELLEN: I mean, not you specifically—

MAY: Sure, cookie—

ELLEN: This may sould, like, I don't know, dumb or something, but for a long time now I've wanted to sleep in the street, you know, like for a night? To see how it feels?

MAY: Yeah?

ELLEN: Yeah.

MAY: Well, the night you do that, honey, you give me the keys to your apartment, 'cause I'll be sleepin' in your bed—

ELLEN: It's no big improvement, believe me—

MAY: Yeah, where ya live?

ELLEN: Amsterdam and 105th

MAY: I sleep in better neighborhoods than that—

ELLEN: I figured—

MAY: Probably you do, too, some nights—

ELLEN: Well that's—

MAY: Like probably whenever you sleep out, it's in a better nighborhood, right, like that's the whole point, huh?

ELLEN: We're supposed to be talking about you.

MAY: Oh, right, my story.

ELLEN: Well, I mean, that sounds ridiculous when you put it like that, I just want to talk.

MAY: Fabulous, sweetheart, fabulous. How much?

ELLEN: How much?

MAY: Yeah.

ELLEN: ...Very much...

MAY: How much are you gonna *pay*?

ELLEN: ...What?

MAY: You can get the whole story for a lump sum—

ELLEN: Are you for real—?

MAY: Or I could charge you per episode—

ELLEN: I don't believe this—

MAY: I figure there's maybe fifteen, sixteen really important episodes in my life; I could give ya each one for like three bucks—

ELLEN: Not one red cent. *(Beat.)*

MAY: *What*?

ELLEN: I'm not paying for some talk—

MAY: This is not *talk*, Cookie—this is the story of my life. 'fI give that away, what've I got left to sell?

ELLEN: *(Starting to leave.)* All right, forget it, I have customers anyway—

MAY: *Wait one goddamn minute—!*

ELLEN: ...What?

MAY: Now, let me get this straight—you are seriously suggestin' that I tell you intimate secrets about myself—

ELLEN: I'm going—

MAY: Which you will use as the basis for charmin' conversation with eligible bachelors who are supposed to marvel at your sensitivity and buy you *presents*?

131

ELLEN: Goodbye.

MAY: And out with this whole profit-makin' situation, I get nothin'?

ELLEN: The manager would like you to leave—

MAY: Screw the manager—

ELLEN: Listen—

MAY: Yeah, yeah, yeah, why'n't you just go wait on those faggots at the next table—that whore and that fag—give them the gift of your presence—

ELLEN: Go—

MAY: Goddamn fuckin' Bloomindale *faggots*—

ELLEN: I'm getting the manager—

MAY: *(Yelling at Peter and Phoebe.)* You stinkin' pigs! *(She hurls her Perrier at them.)* Take *that*, you fuckin' *faggots!*

ELLEN: Listen, you'd better get right out *now* or—

MAY: OR *WHAT? (She turns over the table.)*

ELLEN: I'm getting the manager— *(She exits.)*

THE ECLIPSE
by Joyce Carol Oates
The Washburn apartment - Present - Muriel (76) - Stephanie (36)

Muriel - A woman afraid of growing old
Stephanie - Muriel's daughter

Muriel is an intense, flamboyantly uninhibited woman.
Stephanie is an ardent feminist. She loves her mother but is
frustrated and confused by Muriel's erratic behavior. Here, they
have just returned from grocery shopping. Stephanie berates
Muriel for her embarassing and irrational behavior at the
market.

STEPHANIE *(close to tears, her fear expressed as anger)*: *Why* did
you do that, Mother, when you promised! Why such a—deranged
thing!
MURIEL *(facing audience, back to STEPHANIE: agitated but trying
to appear calm)*: How dare you call me deranged! Who are *you*!
STEPHANIE *(voice raised to be heard over the television)*: Behaving
like that—in *that* store. Now we'll have to get our groceries over at the
A&P on Third Avenue. *(As she sets down her packages, one tips over
and spills several oranges, which, distracted, she stoops to pick up.)*
God damn it, Mother—
MURIEL: I'm Muriel.
STEPHANIE: —you promised.
MURIEL: I—I didn't want them to charge us twice.
STEPHANIE: Nobody was going to charge us twice.
MURIEL *(as if groping)*: It's easy to be cheated in those stores. The
way the check-out woman slides those things along, everything
automatic... *(With increasing anger)* They were watching us. As soon
as we came in, they started. The, what's the word, the surveillance
people—I can sense it.
STEPHANIE *(switching off television)*: Nobody was watching you,
Mother. Why would anyone watch *you*! *(Laughs dispiritedly)*
Behaving the way you do, so entirely unpredictable, dressed like you
are, why would anyone watch *you*!

THE ECLIPSE

MURIEL *(clapping her hands over her ears, dislodging her wig just perceptibly)*: It's too quiet in here suddenly. It isn't natural.

STEPHANIE *(ironically)*: I turned off the television, Mother. Now that we're home we can make our own noises, to scare off burglars.

MURIEL: I don't like too much quiet, my head echoes.

STEPHANIE: You promised you wouldn't act—that way. You promised.

MURIEL: It wasn't "that way"—it was... *(A pause)* another way.

STEPHANIE: There are people who recognize me in those stores— from my picture in the newspaper, from television. I'm so ashamed. *(As the items from the dry cleaner's begin to slide to the floor, STEPHANIE snatches them up and tosses them back down onto the sofa.)* You know better, God damn it. And flirting like that with the butcher—

MURIEL: *He* was flirting with *me*. One of my students from the old days, now he's almost my age—an old man. Y'know why? Because particles speed up as they approach black holes—cross the "event horizon." *(As if warningly)* I don't get any younger but the rest of you get older, fast.

STEPHANIE: That butcher? He was a student of yours?

MURIEL: Look, I had a long teaching career. Half the goddam city— half the goddam *country*—are former students of "Mrs. Washburn," Commodore Stephen Decatur Junior High School. *(Laughs)* There's no escape!

STEPHANIE: And that ridiculous coat of yours—I'm going to throw it away. You've become a clown!

MURIEL *(backing off)*: Oh no you don't. *(Hugs coat tightly about her)*

STEPHANIE: Why did you behave the way you did?

MURIEL: What way?

STEPHANIE: Why did you throw those things on the floor?

MURIEL: I didn't throw them, they fell.

STEPHANIE: Yes? Up over the side of the cart?

MURIEL: Don't you raise your voice to *me*, baby.

STEPHANIE: Then talking so fast. Practically punching me when I

134

touched you.

MURIEL *(pained)*: I—didn't know who it was. Laying hands on me. *(Hesitates)* These icy-cold little hands. Out of nowhere.

STEPHANIE *(incensed)*: Behaving like a madwoman.

MURIEL: Who are you calling a madwoman? *You*—"theorist"!

STEPHANIE: You said you wanted to go shopping—said you were bored at home. And then—you betrayed me.

MURIEL: They're watching you too—with their electronic eyes. Don't think you can escape. *(Defiantly)* Who said I was bored? I'm never bored. Somebody else must've said that.

STEPHANIE: —Losing control like that. In public.

MURIEL *(drawing in a deep breath, pausing, then shrieking)*: I DID NOT LOSE CONTROL! I DO NOT LOSE CONTROL!

(There is a long tense moment: the women stand motionless, perfectly poised. We sense how skillfully MURIEL holds SHEPHANIE in check.)

MURIEL *(calmer, almost conversationally)*: I am *never* bored when alone. I am *only* bored in company.

STEPHANIE *(retreating, taking a package out of one of the grocery bags, murmuring to herself)*: Oh—it's leaking. All over the inside of—

MURIEL: It's just they were watching me. From the first instant I stepped through the—what do you call it— *(Snaps fingers, trying to remember term)* —the seeing-eye door.

STEPHANIE: You cracked the damn thing-the plastic container. *(Peering inside)* "Seafood combo"—\$8.25 a pound. Half of it isn't even real, it's "sea legs." Manufactured in Japan from parts of fish scraps, and dyed pink.

MURIEL *(earnestly)*: Not just watching—I could live with that. I was born in this century. But *taping*. On *microfilm*. Hiding up in the ceiling, the surveillance people. Putting us all on file. *(Hugs herself again in the coat: we see that the pockets are bulging.)*

STEPHANIE: If you're so afraid of people watching you—why the hell make a spectacle of yourself?

MURIEL *(shrewdly)*: To distract them, Stevie. It's an old, old trick of evolution: distracting predators. *(Flaps her arms, mugs, winks toward audience)* First principle of teaching junior high school.

THE ECLIPSE

(MURIEL does a little tap dance, is suprisingly agile.)
STEPHANIE *(close to tears, then reverts to her reproachful tone)*:
Now I can't shop at that Kroger's any more, and the A&P is a mile
away. And you caused such a fuss in the Italian bakery—
MURIEL: It's all in your imagination, we could go back any time.
STEPHANIE: —and the Rexall's. *(Laughs dispiritedly)* If this keeps
up we'll have to move out of the neighborhood.
MURIEL *(as if seriously)*: The elderly provoke the acceleration of
objects in their vicinity: things *fly* into their pockets. Clocks speed up.
Calendars. Pulses.
STEPHANIE: It isn't funny. How can I possibly go to Denver next
month and leave you alone...
MURIEL *(continuing, with eerie precision)*: If—and when—the earth's
density increases its volume must contract, and when its volume
contracts to the size of a pea *(With thumb and forefinger raised
overhead, indicates the size of a pea)*, it will implode—and become a
black hole. And time will cease. And all our problems will be solved.
(A moment's silence. STEPHANIE makes an impatient gesture.)
STEPHANIE: No wonder you scared your students! *(Pause)* When
is *that* going to happen? In a million million years? *(MURIEL shrugs)*
You've been so—almost—sensible—for weeks, and now this. What am
I going to do?
*(MURIEL has drifted off toward stage right, though not in the direction
of her bedroom (at the rear). She has placed her left hand over her left
eye and seems to be testing the vision. As STEPHANIE, not noticing,
carries one of the grocery bags into another room (presumably into the
kitchen, off-stage), MURIEL behaves oddly, removing her hand from her
eye, replacing it quizzically, testing her other eye. (It is the "eclipse"—
a shadow growing in her brain—which she sees or senses.))*
MURIEL: My eye... A blade of—dark.
STEPHANIE *(calling out to her, preoccupied)*: At least take off that
coat. Help me put things away.
MURIEL: Or is it in both eyes? No. Yes...
STEPHANIE: Mother? What is it?
(MURIEL mutters to herself, inaudibly. STEPHANIE approaches her.)

136

THE ECLIPSE

STEPHANIE: Your eye? Your vision? What?

MURIEL: Nothing.

STEPHANIE: Is something wrong? *(STEPHANIE is impeccably well groomed, but at this moment runs a hand through her hair, disheveling it)* —You know your eyes are sensitive to light but you don't protect them. That bright sun—

MURIEL *(with a sudden harsh laugh)*: I'm all right, mind your own business. Your own eyes.

STEPHANIE *(uncertainly)*: Mother, please? Is something wrong?

MURIEL *(muttering as if frightened, defensive)*: Nothing wrong with me, what's wrong with *you*? Always spying on me—the lot of you.

STEPHANIE: Mother—

MURIEL: Who's "Mother"? I'm Muriel.

STEPHANIE: Look—if something is wrong you'd better tell me. I'll make an appointment with Dr. Weisbord.

MURIEL: Oh—hell. Go fly off to Denver, fly off to Paris, or Istanbul, or Hoboken—wherever. Who needs you? I have my own friends.

(STEPHANIE advances upon her but MURIEL wards her off.)

STEPHANIE *(half pleading)*: Mother—should I call Dr. Weisbord. You haven't seen him since July.

MURIEL: Who's "Mother"? You're a feminist, baby, I'm a feminist. Oh boy am *I* a feminist—*I* was there when it was invented. So who's "Mother"?

STEPHANIE: Oh for God's sake, here we go again.

MURIEL *(addressing audience)*: Who gets stuck with "Mother" gets stuck scrubbing the toilets—right?

STEPHANIE *(exasperated)*: You haven't scrubbed a toilet in this apartment in thirty years!

MURIEL: And it looks it, too,

STEPHANIE: *Are* you all right? Just tell me.

MURIEL *(takes a hand mirror out of her pocket, shoves it in STEPHANIE's face in a brusque gesture)*: Look at yourself, baby, not me. You're the Ph.D. You're the professor. You pay the bills around here, not me.

137

THE ECLIPSE

(STEPHANIE flinches from the sight of her own reflection, oddly; then renews her tack.)

STEPHANIE; I'd better call Dr. Weisbord.

MURIEL *(quickly)*: The problem is—you're ashamed of me. Of your own dear mother, ashamed. "Prominent Feminist Ashamed of Her Own Dear Mother."

STEPHANIE: I am not—ashamed. I'm worried.

MURIEL: "I'm worried!"

STEPHANIE *(clutching MURIEL's wrist, trying to hold her still so she can look into MURIEL's eyes)*: Don't mock me, please. It isn't you. It's—that other person.

(A pause. MURIEL disengages herself, with an air of dignity.)

STEPHANIE: The way you lost control in the store—it wasn't you was it?

MURIEL *(defiantly):* I told you: I didn't want those crooks to charge us twice.

STEPHANIE: God damn it, Mother—you know it's just routine, they staple the, the *(She becomes nervous, rattled, speaking rapidly)* receipts to the bags—from the deli counter—you know that. *(Locates one of the bags, with a stapled receipt, to show to MURIEL, who airily ignores it.)* Nobody was going to make us pay twice. And even if, if— if they tried to—why throw things onto the *floor?* Like a madwoman?

MURIEL *(contemptuously)*: What do you—*you!*—know about madness!

(A pause. MURIEL changes tone, reverts to her flamboyant, stagey self. From this point until the end of the scene, the lights should dim at the periphery of the action, focussing upon MURIEL and STEPHANIE, with MURIEL at the center, as if greedy for attention.)

MURIEL: She who lasts, laughs. *(She pats one of her deep pockets, pulls out an item—a box of gourmet chocolates; professes surprise)* Why—what have we here? *(Out of that same pocket, she pulls a jar of fancy cocktail shrimp)* Uh-oh—what's this? *(Out of another pocket, a mango)* And this?

(STEPHANIE is utterly astonished, watching with wide childlike eyes. A strand of hair has fallen into her face and her posture is less assured

than it was only a few minutes ago.)

STEPHANIE: Oh my God, Mother—what have you done?

MURIEL *(winking at audience)*: Who's "Mother"? I'm Muriel.

STEPHANIE: But-when did you take those things? How? I was watching you every second.

MURIEL *(chuckling)*: Now you see it: voilà! Now you don't! *(A small jar of caviar in the palm of her hand, then disappearing up her sleeve)*

STEPHANIE: How could you! I trusted you!

MURIEL: Treat time for my little girl! Things you can't afford on your salary!

STEPHANIE *(growing angry)*: I'll have to take those things back to the store.

MURIEL: What?

STEPHANIE: Back to the store. Right now. *(Half sobbing)* Oh—I should have known better. God damn it I should have known.

MURIEL: Oh no you're not baby. These're *mine*.

(MURIEL tosses the mango to STEPHANIE, who has no choice but to catch it. She laughs, rather shrilly.)

STEPHANIE *(sadly)*: It's all a joke to you now, isn't it?

MURIEL: What's a joke? *(Sniffs under an arm)* Where?

STEPHANIE: Life. *(Speaking slowly, not quite accusingly)* The life remaining to you.

MURIEL: Nah—I'm imbued with the "tragic sense of life," you betcha. Teach in any American public school for forty years, it's natural.

STEPHANIE: Now I have to take these things back. These—God—damned—*things*. *(Quietly furious. It is evident that STEPHANIE is deflecting her deep concern for MURIEL's health along lines of a more conventionaly emotional exasperation, disgust. She picks up the items flamboyantly, wiping tears from her eyes.)* God *damn*, and *damn*, and *damn*.

MURIEL: Aw Stevie where's your sense of humor? *(Snatches one of the items from her, drops it in her pocket.)*

STEPHANIE: Give that back! Mother—damn *you*!

THE ECLIPSE

MURIEL *(less certainly)*: Hey—Stevie?

STEPHANIE: Don't call me that ridiculous name, I hate it!

MURIEL: Don't yell at me, baby. *(As STEPHANIE snatches at one of the items)* These things're *mine*. LOOT.

(A brief inffectual scuffle. STEPHANIE, though furious, sobbing in frustration, is timid about using force against her mother. When a jar falls to the floor she give a little scream and kicks it off stage. By this time only the two women are fully illuminated.)

MURIEL *(hands over ears; repentant; perhaps genuinely frightened)*: Baby—why are you crying? I, I won't do it again—I promise. *(Pause)* I won't go shopping with you again.

STEPHAINE *(wiping face, calmer)*: That's why I'm crying, Mother— you won't go shopping with me again. Today was the last time.

(LIGHTS DARKEN. WOMEN stand motionless. As lights go out:)

MURIEL *(with bravado)*: Who's "Mother"? I'm Muriel.

(LIGHTS OUT.)

THE HAVE-LITTLE
by Migdalia Cruz
South Bronx - 1974-1976 - Lillian (13-15) - Carmen (38-40)

Lillian - A Puerto Rican girl, innocent and spiritual
Carmen - Lillian's mother, mostly exhausted by life

Here, Carmen takes out her frustrations on her daughter, Lillian.

(CARMEN stands over LILLIAN. SHE is in a rage.)
CARMEN: *(Grabbing LILLIAN's arm)* Answer me when I ask you something!
LILLIAN: *(Pulling away from CARMEN)* You're hurting my arm.
(CARMEN slaps LILLIAN)
CARMEN: A lot more than that will hurt Miss! Take off your clothes!
LILLIAN: No, Mami! Please!
CARMEN: Don't make me rip them off your body! You want me to hit you? I don't want to! Don't make me act like your father! Don't make me treat you like an animal! *(SHE pulls off LILLIAN's sweater, THEY struggle.)* Let me see your arms.
LILLIAN: *(Holding out her arms.)* I din't do nuffin!
CARMEN: I bet you did something with him. Tell me. Tell me what you did with that garbage. *(SHE holds LILLIAN's face in her hands)* Tell me the truth.
LILLIAN: I tole you the truth. He had respect for me.
CARMEN: *(Letting go of her face)* Respect?! What do you know about that? *(SHE slaps her)* There's some respect! *(SHE looks at LILLIAN)* You don't know respect! *(SHE pulls at LILLIAN's blouse)* Take them all off.
LILLIAN: *(Struggling with her)* Why do you want to hurt me?
CARMEN: *(Reaching beneath LILLIAN's skirt)* You let him touch you.
LILLIAN: No! Mami, don't! He din't touch me there. He never touched me. Stop it! Please, stop! I love you!
(SHE moves away from LILLIAN)
CARMEN: You disgraced me! How could you do that to me?
LILLIAN: I din't do nuffin.

141

CARMEN: Tell me the truth! Tell me or get out of this house. Tell me!

LILLIAN: Please! I don't wanna go no where else!

CARMEN: Then tell me everything!

LILLIAN: There ain't nuffin to tell. I swear!

CARMEN: Is that what you want? You want me to kick you out?! *(Pause)* I can't stand to look at you.

INÉS DE CASTRO
by John Clifford
A castle in Portugal - 16th Century - Inés (30's) - Nurse (40-50)

Inés - The Spanish mistress of the Crown Prince of Portugal
Nurse - Ines' servant

Based on an historical incident, this is the tale of a proud woman
whose life was forfeit as a result of escalating hostilities between
Spain and Portuagal in the 16th century. Inés loves the Prince
beyond reason, and this love will cost her everything, as can be
seen in the following confrontaiton with her faithful old nurse.

INÉS: I'm sorry.
NURSE: And you tell me nothing ever happened.
INÉS: I wasn't thinking.
NURSE: You never think!
INÉS: I want to live! That's all I ever wanted. And they all hated me
and wanted me dead.
NURSE: You shouldn't say such things. You should be ashamed.
INÉS: It's true.
NURSE: They never did. No one would want such a wicked thing.
INÉS: Will you stop cleaning!
NURSE: The floor's dirty.
INÉS: I don't care!
NURSE: And besides someone's coming.
INÉS: Who?
NURSE: I've forgotten. You got me all upset.
INÉS: I didn't mean to.
NURSE: You weren't to know. It all happened before you were born.
I just cleaned for your father then. Until the day your mother died and
I found myself holding you. You were so tiny. And I said to myself
don't touch her. Don't. Put her down. They'll only take advantage.
And they did. But I couldn't. I couldn't put you down. You were so
tiny. So helpless. All I wanted was to keep you safe. I swore I'd
protect you. A fine mess I've made of it.
INÉS: You have not.

INÉS DE CASTRO

NURSE: I have so. Look at you. Among all these foreigners. These Portuguese. They hate you more than your own folk ever did. I wish we were home.

INÉS: No. I'm glad I left. Glad! We've been happy.

NURSE: It won't last.

INÉS: Why not?

NURSE: Never trust a man. He'll go and die on you. They all do. They just go and die on you out of spite.

INÉS: He's not like that.

NURSE: They're in love with death, the lot of them. Death is their companion. Death their friend. I've watched them. When they pray to the lady in the chapel it's not for safety but for strength. For the courage to meet death in the eye and never falter. That's what they pray for. All of them. Not for life. Not for love. But for a good death. And they're all the same. You've been happy with yours but you'll pay for it.

INÉS: I don't care what it costs.

NURSE: Well you should.

INÉS: How can you say such things. You helped us.

NURSE: You were fretting yourself to pieces. And he had a way with him.

INÉS: He looked at me like no one else. Not like an object or a piece of meat. Not like a jewel or the fulfilment of a dream. Not like the men my father always pushed at me. With their greedy faces and their groping hands. The ones I was meant to marry. Marry to conclude some alliance or cement some deal. All of them were liars. Brave sometimes with their swords, but cowards with their inner selves. Inept useless cowards. He wasn't like that at all. Not the one I chose. I knew it, the minute I saw him I knew it, and I wanted him.

NURSE: He was married.

INÉS: That's never been a marriage. You know that. It was just politics. He never loved her. She never gave him children. They were never happy. They've never laughed. Not like us.

NURSE: You used to laugh together the whole night long. I never got a wink of sleep.

INÉS DE CASTRO

INÉS: You never wanted to sleep!
NURSE: You'd walk by the sea and the waves would never touch you. But now the tide is lapping at your feet. It had to. It was madness.
INÉS: It was joy. Joy for both of us.

JULIET AND SUE
from <u>Making It</u>
by Douglas Taylor
Midwestern Town - Present - Juliet (40's-50's) - Sue (40's-50's)

Juliet - A skittish and defensive newcomer
Sue - A town "maven"

Sue has invited Juliet over for the evening because their
husbands are on a hunting trip together. Juliet's husband
desperately wants them to belong. Juliet, on the other hand,
feels trapped and unhappy in this tightly bound community
where everyone knows each others business. Here, in an
attempt to get her to loosen up, Sue persuades Juliet to have a
nightcap, and gets more than she bargained for.

JULIET: *(Looking room over, suspiciously)* This is a pleasant room.
SUE: Why thank you. Would you like a fire? I could light it.
JULIET: It's not like all the other front rooms in Dry Gulch.
SUE: Dry Gulch?
JULIET: Dead Man's End. This room remembers something. *(A sudden challenge)* What?
(SUE, who is at bar, stops, has an uneasy moment, goes on)
SUE: You didn't say whether you wanted a drink or not.
JULIET: No.
SUE: Oh. I rather hoped you would... What I mean is—Fred and I usually have a night cap together.
(JULIET turns sharply but there is not sharpness is her tone)
JULIET: Something Ginny and tall.
SUE: *(Pleasantly surprised)* Then you want one?
JULIET: *(Moving about the room again)* Have you always lived here?
SUE: *(Working on drinks)* Heavens no, Fred and I used to live over on Elm Street before things...started paying off. Pre-Fred, I was a buyer for a millinery store in Topeka, Kansas.
JULIET: Topeka, Kan.
SUE: Yes, it was a heavenly job. Twice a year I was sent to New York on buying sprees, all expenses paid. How about gin and tonic?

146

JULIET AND SUE

JULIET: And that's where you met Freddy—in New York?

SUE: Yes! Who told you? Billy? One of the girls?

JULIET: I met Billy, in New Jersey.

SUE: Oh? *(SHE mixes drinks.)*

JULIET: *(English accent)* Really, now—you're not going to ask me about meeting Billy in New Jersey?

SUE: Ask you? Should I?

JULIET: And I thought you would be above 'games'.

SUE: Above games? That depends on the sort of games. I've read articles by psychologists that maintain that all we ever do is...play games. It's all a sort of game. What game?

JULIET: *(A bit melodramatically)* The game of...'pretending'.

SUE: Pretending?

JULIET: My dear Mrs. Wade fess up—there is an ulterior.

SUE: Ulterior.

JULIET: Motive.

SUE: Motive?

JULIET: To all *this*.

SUE: There is?

JULIET: All evening, at the club, we've been chatting about this and that, never getting down to brass tacks. I drive you home, you invite me in, not for a drink but to get down to brass tacks.

SUE: Perhaps.

JULIET: You don't lie, do you?

SUE: Of course, I don't lie, it just depends, actually it really all depends on what you mean by 'brass tacks'.

JULIET: You're on an assignment.

SUE: Am I?

JULIET: Your mission is to find out 'all about' Juliet Need—who she is, what she is, and report it back to the girls... *(With a flurry)* 'Les Girls!' *(Speaks as if addressing a women's club)* After all, girls, Juliet Need has been among us for several months now and we know very little about her. She seems a bit...offish. And before welcoming her with open arms into the closed social circle of Poison Arrow, we must know what to expect from her. Is she dependable? That is, will she

147

hold up in the long run, this question mark William has dropped into our midsts? Is she sturdy, upright, morally our equal? After all, word has it that she was an actress at one time and you know what they say about actressess!

SUE: What do they say about actresses?

JULIET: It would be simpler to tell you what they don't say about actresses. *(SUE hands her her drink)* What's this?

SUE: What is it I'm supposed to ask you about your meeting Billy in New Jersey?

JULIET: Good Christ-in-the-morning, do I have to do it for you?

SUE: *(After a pause)* Unfortunately, there is very little that people have to do for me. *(JULIET looks at her for a long moment. Takes the drink.)* The girls *are* quite anxious to know about you.

JULIET: And you were the obvious choice since you were in millinery with an expense account. 'Consequently'—when Freddy mentioned at breakfast one morning that he and Billy and some of the fellas, 'Les boys', were going bear hunting on the weekend and prove they still got their 'you know whats', you said, musingly, 'hmmmmmmmm, that just may be a peachy time for Juliet Need and myself to get together for a get acquainted evening', and good old bear hunting, dead-eyed Fred, said—'say, honey, good idea.' *(SUE just laughs. Toasting)* To your mission.

SUE: *(Smiling, watching her)* To my mission.

(THEY both drink. JULIET taking a rather large gulp. SHE reacts violently, coughing, fanning her mouth)

JULIET: Jesus, you trying to find me out or destroy me!?

SUE: Oh, is it too strong? If you like—I'll dilute it for you.

JULIET: *(Turns away, ignoring her)* Poor Billy. Poor shoot-the-bear-in-the-ass-and-win-a-cigar Billy. *(Sips drink)* He was so nervous about this girly get together of ours. He really wants me to make it with you. Make the scene, with *you* and *all* the ladies of Dodge City. The social set of Bad Man's Gulch. That marvelous, delicious little dirty-faced fish woman on Clark Street that I have a ball buying shrimp from on Tuesday and Friday, he doesn't give a hoot about, but you Susan Wade and your team of...Alaskan huskies... *(Slight laugh,*

JULIET AND SUE

studying the drink as if if were a pool of mystery and then sips it) Mustn't blame him. After all, your Freddy is more or less in charge of the town and if a guy wants to get ahead like Billy does... *(Sips drink again, treating it a little like an eleven year old treats an ice cream cone)* Did they check me out with the FBI?

SUE: Hardly.

JULIET: Just as well. I'm clean in the Commie department.

SUE: Juliet, I honestly think that you misunderstand...

JULIET: *(Holding drink up to the light)* Your method's pretty obvious...obvious, you know that?

SUE: Juliet, dear...

JULIET: Oh, come on, *huh*—let's drop the crap-front.

SUE: You're much too suspicious of me, I'm not a member of the C.I.A.

JULIET: The hell you're not—you're a snoop if I ever saw one.

SUE: Perhaps I'd better dilute that drink...

JULIET: You stay away from my drink. It's all highly deducible. I deduced your purpose. Now I'll deduce your method.

SUE: You're incorrigible.

JULIET: Surreptitious inebriation.

SUE: What?

JULIET: Your method. Surreptitious inebriation.

SUE: I swear to you...

JULIET: At dinner—at the club—I refuse liquor. Unconcerned, you quietly down *three* martinis.

SUE: You kept count?

JULIET: You referred to me as the 'mysterious abstainer'. Tauntingly! Deny that.

SUE: I can't.

JULIET: *But*—once you lured me...

SUE: *Lured*?

JULIET: Lured me into the interrogation room...

SUE: *Interrogation* room! *(Laughs)* Oh, my dear...

JULIET: You sneak me a block-buster.

SUE: *Sneaked* you a ...

149

JULIET AND SUE

JULIET: *Sneaked*. Sneak, sneaked, snucked. Anyway you conjugate it, it spells 'surreptitious inebriation'.

SUE: *(With laughter)* Oh, dear...

JULIET: Get the suspect greased and she'll reveal all.

SUE: This is much too melodramatic for me.

JULIET: Wanna know something screwy?—probably it's gonna work. Know why? There's one thing I'd hate to do, one thing I'd *really* hate to do—disappoint the celestial Social Hierach of *(Loudly. Glass raised high)* Rattle Snake Canyon! And the boys at the hunting lodge! *(About to drink)* The darlings. *(Swallows deep. Her head goes back and stays there so SHE is looking up at the ceiling and the effect of the liquor seems to seep into her fibres)* Hey... Hey, now...Oooooooooooo screw... Scr-rew...*IT!* Have a ball! Have yourself a big fat over-delayed over due ball. And know what first? For starters? Call up the boys. Call up the boys at Coon Skin Lodge or wherever the hell they are and give 'em a big wifey hello. *(Crosses toward the phone)*

SUE: Do you think that would be wise?

JULIET: Wise? Who cares if it's wise or not? *(Picks up phone, speaks, not bothering to dial)* Hello, Billy..? Billy-illy? Hello, you sweet loveable fuzzy-haired old pussy cat you, how's the bear murdering campaign coming along? You haven't gone hunting yet? Aww... It's night and you and the boys only just arrived? Well, listen sweety-kums, I just called...to tell you before you got loaded...that I miss you... Yeah...I miss you where it hurts most, 'cause, you know why, Billy? 'Cause it's a full moon out and I feel awful amorous, and, and, and honey?—you'd better just hop into the Chevy and get your sweet ass back here 'cause I'm about to go down and lay the whole goddamn police force! *(Slams down receiver, crosses)* Try telling that one at Hazel Lopert's bridge party next Wednesday. *(SUE smiles)* Stop smiling, you smiling Machiavellian... Hellion. *(SHE crosses to the sofa, sits)*

SUE: You flatter me.

JULIET: The hell I do. *(A moment and then SHE lets herself fall out flat on the sofa)* Oh Jesus. *(One arm hungs down to the floor, the glass in her hand. SUE rises, takes the glass, crosses up to the bar,*

150

JULIET AND SUE

speaks as SHE pours)
SUE: I know what you are experiencing. I know it like one knows an old familiar but now distant friend. Familiar—because one never forgets. Distant—it was a long time ago. I made my peace thank God. And you'll make yours. I know you quite well, pie-face. You see, I was you—a very long time ago. And therefore—I know the pain you live with. I'll prove it to you, if you wish. Why not? *(Announces)* "People who sever the magnetic chain of human society, experience intense and often-times unbearable pain". *(Looks down at the drinks for a moment, begins)* When I first arrived in this town of many names, I was very much the free spirit determined not to be fettered, alla promethius, by a small town ingrown narrow-minded snobbish self-destructive indolent society of prissy women. I was stubbornly determined. Yes...stubbornly determined. *(Thinks for a moment—goes on)* Fred, a well established member of the inner circle—the oppostion —had other plans. Plans that had nothing to do with preserving the freedom of the soul. Seeing what was afoot, he set out, quickly and systematically, to nudge me into the main stream. He was gentle at first, very gentle. He tried cajoling, begging, and getting nowhere— resorted to despotism, ordering me to join up. But I was young and strong and held my ground. Then toward the end of my third month of stubborn, stoic determination—you've been here about that long haven't you? *(JULIET moves, slightly. SUE continues, unaware of JULIET's movement)* I suddenly found myself doing strange things, all sorts of stange things like sticking my tongue out and snarling at people behind their backs and right at Fred's face. The poor darling was so confused. What had he married? Oh my dear, he made remarks, accusations that were...far from flattering to my femininity. I later forgave him. If only I had had an ally. But I was alone and without an ally. As you are. Yes, I was alone all that summer, through the fall, the autumn and in the winter I succumbed...gave in. I know the pain you are experiencing. 'People who sever the magnetic chain of human society experience intense and often-times unbearable pain'. Q.E.D. *(SHE crossses to sofa and holds out JULIET's drink. JULIET's muffled voice can be heard, coming from under pillows.)*

151

JULIET AND SUE

JULIET: Bull... *(Another silence, during which SUE says nothing. Then JULIET scrambles to her feet and faces SUE)* You don't know me, you don't know me—what I am, what I feel, what I do or don't, can or can't, have or have not endured! You think I'm an amateur? My freshman year at college, I was the hottest sorority pledge on campus. They all wanted me, all 'les Girls' wanted me to be a member of them. There were five damned sororities and one frat that pledged me that year. It was a wild relentless month of teas and dances and special dinners and finally the time came for me to decide. Which one? And after considerable thought, this is what I did. I gave a tea of my own to which I invited *all* the presidents of *all* the sororities. Naturally, they came—each expecting to be the only gaddamned sorority president present.   The   looks   of   disappointment   were   heartbreaking, heartbreaking. But they had youth, they had resiliency, they adapted and the tea went on and hope again surged and then at the height of tea drinking I rose and stood before them. Oh, I can still see those sweet, sweet, hope-filled, innocent faces smiling up at me as I said—'Girls, I have made my decision; here is my answer to your gracious offers.' *(SHE points the index finger of her right hand and raises her arm to its full length, making a raspberry sound with her lips and tongue. A moment passes before SUE speaks)*
SUE: That's an interesting story.
JULIET: There's only one thing wrong with it.
SUE: What's that?
JULIET: I didn't go to college.

LETTICE & LOVAGE
by Peter Shaffer
England - Present - Lettice (40's-50's) - Lotte (40's)

Lettice - An imaginative tour guide
Lotte - Lettice's boss

Lettice Doufett is a highly imaginative and romantic woman with
a flair for the dramatic. She exploits these qualities daily in her
job as a tour guide at Fustian House, a sixteenth century English
manor house. She embellishes her speeches to the tour groups
with her own exciting interpretations of the family's history.
Here, Lotte proceeds to fire an outraged Lettice.

LOTTE: Ah, Miss Douffet, good afternoon. Please sit down.
(LETTICE sits in a chair facing LOTTE.) I hope you had a pleasant
journey up to London.
LETTICE: That is not very likely, is it?—considering one is about to
be arraigned.
LOTTE: I'm sorry?
LETTICE: I'm at the Bar of Judgment, am I not?
LOTTE: Your position is to be reviewed, actually. I'm sure you see
the inevitability of that. I have no choice in the matter.
LETTICE: Like the headsman.
LOTTE: I'm sorry?
LETTICE: The headsman always asked forgiveness of those he was
about to decapitate.
LOTTE: I would really apprecialte it if we could exclude historical
analogies from this conversation.
LETTICE: As you please.
LOTTE: It is, after all, solely to do with your job and your fitness to
perform it. We both know what we have to talk about. As an official
of the department which employs you I cannot possibly overlook what
I witnessed yesterday afternoon. I cannot understand it, and I cannot
possibly condone it. Do you have anything to say in extenuation?
(A pause.)
LETTICE: It is not my fault.

153

LETTICE & LOVAGE

LOTTE: I'm sorry?

LETTICE: Except in a most limited sense of that word.

LOTTE: Then whose is it?

LETTICE: I respect accuracy in recounting history when it is moving and startling. Then I would not dream altering a single detail.

LOTTE: That is gracious of you.

LETTICE: In some cases, however, I do confess I feel the need to take a hand... I discovered this need working at Fustian House this summer. It is wholly the fault of that house that I yielded to it.

LOTTE: Of the house?

LETTICE: Yes.

LOTTE: You are actually blaming the house for those grotesque narrations?

LETTICE: I am. Most definitely. Fustian House is quite simply the *dullest house in England*! If it has any rival in that category I have yet to discover it... It is actually *impossible* to make interesting! Not only is its architecture in the very gloomiest style of Tudor building, *nothing whatever happened in it!—over four hundred years*! A queen almost fell downstairs—but didn't! A girl did fall—not even downstairs—and survivied to be honored by the poor. How am I expected to make anything out of that?

LOTTE: You are not expected to make things *out* of the house, Miss Douffet. Merely to show people *around* it.

LETTICE: I'm afraid I can't agree. I am there to enlighten them. That first of all.

LOTTE: Enlighten?

LETTICE: Light them up! "Enlarge! Enliven! Enlighten!" That was my mother's watchword. She called them the three Es. She was a great teacher, my mother.

LOTTE: Really? At what institution?

LETTICE: The oldest and best. The Theatre. *(MISS SHOEN bristles.)* All good actors are instructors, as I'm sure you realize.

LOTTE: *(Cold)* I'm afraid I don't at all.

LETTICE: But certainly! "Their subject is Us— Their sources are Themselves!" —Again, my mother's phrase. She ran a touring

company of players, all trained by her to speak Shakespeare thrillingly
in the French tongue.

LOTTE: The French?

LETTICE: Yes. She moved to France after the war, unable to find
employment in her native England equal in the Dordogne. It was not
really very appreciative of Shakespeare.

LOTTE: The French peasantry is hardly noted for that kind of
enthusiasm, I understand.

LETTICE: Nor the intellectuals either. Voltaire called Shakespeare
barbare, did you know that? Barbarian.

LOTTE: I'm not surprised. The Gallic mind imagines it invented
civilization.

LETTICE: My mother set out to correct that impression. Her
company was called, in pure defiance, "Les Barbares"!

LOTTE: She was evidently not afraid of challenge.

LETTICE: Never! Every girl was trained to phrase faultlessly.

LOTTE: And every man also, one presumes.

LETTICE: There were no men.

LOTTE: You mean it was an all-girl company?

LETTICE: Indeed. My mother married a Free French soldier in
London called Douffet, who abandoned her within three months of the
wedding. She had no pleasure thereafter in associating with
Frenchmen. "They are all fickle," she used to say. "Fickle and
furtive."

LOTTE: A fair description of the whole nation, I would say.

LETTICE: She brought me up entirely by herself. Mainly on the road.
We played all over the Dordogne—in farmhouses and barns, wherever
they would have us. We performed only the history plays of
Shakespeare, because history was my mother's passion. I was the stage
manager, responsible for costumes, props, and sword fights. Fights, I
may say, as ferocious as they can only be, enacted by a horde of Gallic
girls in armor when their dander is really up! She herself was famous
for her King Richard the Third. She used to wear a pillow on her back
as a hump. It was brilliantly effective. *(Springing up)* No one who
heard it will ever forget the climax of her performance—the cry of total

155

despair wrung from her on the battlefield! *(Stooping, to imitate the royal hunchback)* "Un cheval! Un cheval! Mon royaume pour un cheval!" *(LOTTE stares astounded.)* All the translations were her own.

LOTTE: A remarkable achievement.

LETTICE: Not for her. Language was her other passion. As I grew up I was never permitted to read anything but the grandest prose. "Language alone frees one," she used to say. "And History gives one place." She was adamant I should not lose my English heritage, either of words or deeds. Every night she enacted for me a story from our country's past, fleshing it out with her own marvelous virtuosity!... Richard's battlefield of Bosworth, with the golden crown hung up in a thornbush! King Charles the First marching to his beheading like a ramrod on a freezing January morning, wearing two shirts of snowy white linen, lest if he trembled from cold his enemies would say it was from fear!... *(Rapt)* Wonderful!... On a child's mind the most tremendous events were engraved as with a diamond on a windowpane!... And to me, my tourists—simply random holidaymakers in my care for twenty minutes of their lives—are *my* children in this respect. It is my duty to enlarge them. Enlarge—enliven—enlighten them.

LOTTE: With fantasies?

LETTICE: Fantasy floods in where fact leaves a vacuum.

LOTTE: Another saying of your mother's?

LETTICE: My own!... When I first went to Fustian House I spoke nothing *but* fact! Exactly what was set down for me—in all its glittering excitement. By the time I'd finished, my whole group would have turned gray with indifference. I myself turned gray every afternoon!... Fustian is a Haunted House, Miss Schoen. Haunted by the Spirit of Nullity! Of Nothing Ever Happening!... It had to be fought.

LOTTE: With untruth.

LETTICE: With anything!

LOTTE: *(Implacably)* With untruth.

LETTICE: *(Grandly)* I am the daughter of Alice Evans Douffet— dedicated to lighting up the world, not dousing it in dust! My tongue simply could not go on speaking that stuff!... No doubt it was excessive. I was carried—I can't deny it—further and further from the shore of fact down the slipstream of fiction. But blame the house—not the spirit which defied it!

LOTTE: And this is your defense?

LETTICE: Where people once left yawning they now leave *admiring*. I use that word in its strict old sense—meaning a State of Wonder. That is no mean defense.

LOTTE: It is completely irrelevant!

LETTICE: Last month I put out a soup-bowl by the rear exit. Not from greed—though heaven knows I could forgiven that, with what you pay me. I wanted *proof*! People express gratitude the same way all over the world: with their money. *(Proudly)* My soup-bowl *brims*! It brims every evening with their coins, as they themselves are brimming! I watch them walking away afterwards to the car park, and those are *Brimming People*. Every one!

LOTTE: *(Tartly)* Really? If you were to look through these letters you might discover quite a few who were not actually brimming—except with indignation.

(LETTICE approaches the desk and examines a letter.)

LETTICE: Churls are always with us. Curmudgeons are never slow to come forward.

LOTTE: *(Furious) Twenty-two letters*! I have twenty-two letters about you, Miss Douffet!... None them exactly written in a state of wonder!

LETTICE: *(Loftily)* Twenty-two—what's *that*?... I have fifty—sixty! Here—look for yourself! Here!... Behold!... Here!

(She grabs her satchel and empties its contents over the desk—a small avalanche of envelopes.) Vox populi! The Voice of the People!... I wrote my address beside my soup-bowl. This is the result!

LOTTE: *(Protesting)* Please, Miss Douffet!... This is my desk!

LETTICE: *(Hotly)* Read them. Read for yourself!... *There* is my defense. The Voice of the People!... Read!

LOTTE: *(Exploding) I will not! I will not!* This is nonsense—all of it! They don't matter!... None of this matters—your mother—your childhood—your car park—*I don't care! (Pause; struggling to control herself)* I am not in the entertainment business—and nor are you. That is all. We are guarding a heritage. Not running a theater. That is all.

157

MIRIAM'S FLOWERS
by Migdalia Cruz
Bronx - 1975 - Delfina (30-40) - Miriam (16)

Delfina - A woman struggling to cope with the death of her
young son
Miriam - Delfina's troubled daughter

Delfina and Miriam both grieve for little Puli in their own ways.
Here, Delfina seeks a moment of closeness with Miriam and
tells her a bedtime story like she used to do when Miriam was
little. Miriam destroys the mood, however, by attacking
Delfina's lover, Nando.

*(DELFINA pretends to read from a children's Bible book to MIRIAM,
who is in bed, shaking.)*
DELFINA: Miriam lived in the desert. She had a very big heart. She
had ten brothers. She followed Moses around and he would have
married her except he couldn't get into the promised land. So she
married somebody else. *(Closes the book firmly)* Go to sleep now!
MIRIAM: Mami!
DELFINA: You're almost sixteen years old, Miriam. The only thing
you should be scared of is outside—on the street. Go to sleep.
MIRIAM: Why didn't Miriam marry Moses? It seems like a good
match and everything.
DELFINA: Because he was ugly. And short. A short, ugly, dark
man.
MIRIAM: Like Nando.
DELFINA: Nando is beautiful. Didn't you ever look at his lips. They
are—they are like chocolate baby twins.
MIRIAM: He's short though. Do he ever act funny around water?
DELFINA: What do you mean?
MIRIAM: Like do he do Moses—like things?
DELFINA: No.
MIRIAM: He don't talk much.
DELFINA: He's only got half a tongue.
MIRIAM: What do you mean? Like somebody cut it out?

DELFINA: Yeah. When he was a little boy.

MIRIAM: No shit! That's somefin... He probably don' kiss too good then.

DELFINA: He kisses great.

MIRIAM: Moses couldn'ta been as short as Nando.

DELFINA: Why not? Everybody was shorter then. They had to run around and carry stuff across the desert, so they had to be low to the ground.

MIRIAM: Shit. I'm glad I don' live in those times. I like tall guys.

DELFINA: Go to sleep! *(DELFINA turns off the light and exits to kitchen)*

MIRIAM: Shit! I like 'em tall. With dark, wavy hair and no hair on they backs or shoulders cause I want to vomit when I feel that kind of hair. *(A loud whisper)* And with dicks that you can see when they're walking— The kind that gets in their legs' way and they gotta keep shifting it around because it bothers them. I love those kind cause they need somebody to take care of it for them... Why do she always gotta turn off the light?

159

ONE-ACT PLAY
by Yannick Murphy
Rural America - Present - Mama (40's) - Alix (13)

Mama - A woman struggling to keep her family together
Alix - Mama's young daughter

When her son locks himself in her bedroom, Mama talks to Alix
in the kitchen. Alix is teaching herself palmistry, and tries to
convince her mother that when she gets the hang of it, it will
become a lucrative career.

ALIX: You tell that Fred Garber to mind his own business. He ain't
my father.
MAMA: Girl where have you been?
ALIX: Don't you think I'm too old to be pulled by the hair?
MAMA: Who pulled your hair?
ALIX: *(Alix uses a softer voice, her attention diverted.)* He still in
there? *(pointing at the door Ray's behind.)*
MAMA: How'd it look if I put this rug in front of the door?
ALIX: Maybe he's dead. Y'ever think of that?
MAMA: Whenever he's outta my sight. Ever since he was a baby.
ALIX: Maybe he's fulfillin' your fear for you. 'Cause deep inside
your fear is what you really want.
MAMA: I don't know what you're talkin' about. Got something to do
with palms? Anyway, I'm gonna put this on the front porch instead.
I'm not gonna let us look like the town gypsies like your father left us
to look like.
ALIX: Just think, it would put an end to all the worrying, one less
mouth to feed. Take a look at the pot, soup never lasted two days
before.
MAMA: Fred couldn't do it. I'm beginnin' to think I was dreamin'
when I saw him lift Kleppa.
ALIX: That's what fear's all about. It's the thing you want the most.
That's why Rosemary was so scared tonight, I tell you Mama she
wouldn't sit down with me, she wouldn't let me read her. She didn't
want to know the truth about the future. I could see plain from where

160

she was sittin', though, she's gonna leave Joe Thompson, plain as day. I could see it all in the reflection of that big mirror Garsha's got in the back of the bar. I couldda told her how to prepare for it all.

MAMA: Garsha's! You been at Garsha's all this time while there's been a crisis going on in here?

ALIX: *(Looking at the rug)* Yeah, green. He'll love it. I'd call that a regular catastrophic decision to make, somethin' akin to a family crisis. *(Mama turns away, goes to kitchen and pulls out flour from cupboard, starts rolling it to make more noodle soup.)* You told me somethin' once, Mama, how when we were little you took us and Joan's kids to the supermarket with you, and there were so many of us that when you got back in the truck and counted heads, you musta miscounted cause half way to the house you realized Ray wasn't in the car, and your first feeling was of relief that you didn't have to hustle him into the house also and pull off his snowsuit, along with the rest of us, your first thought was how much easier it would be with only five kids clothes to pull off and hands to warm. It wasn't until your second thought that you panicked and turned around to get him.

MAMA: That's different. I was teasin' you kids. It's like what I told you about the paperbag, how I found you in a paper bag on the street and took you home cause I felt sorry for you. Just a joke Alix. A family joke. *(Angry)* Christ, why am I standin' here defendin' myself when I can't sleep at night cause he's locked himself in there? I'm the only one pickin' rugs to lighten this place up, to make it work. I don't need your holier than thou talk. Get outta my sight, go to your room and leave me alone.

ALIX: Just like you know he's behind that door, you know I'm behind mine. You ain't gonna make me go away. *(Mama runs into the bathroom, slams the door but door doesn't shut, she knocks toilet seat down, sits on it, pulls tissue from the roller to wipe her nose. Alix stands in the doorway. Yelling)* Why you actin' so dumb? You knew he was gonna leave you. Whole town knew it. You knew it would just be the three of us. You wanted it this way, didn't you? You wanted to be the one to make all the decisions, to run our lives all by yourself.

MAMA: Alix that ain't true.

ALIX: Just stop your cryin'. I know you can stop your cryin', you

161

just want me to feel sorry for you, cause you think it's all on your shoulders to save him. Well he ain't a baby in a snowsuit anymore, he can get up and walk around anywhere he wants to, and he's gonna do it without your sayso. Get it straight Mama. I don't feel any pity for you.

(In the meantime, during their yelling, Ray has come out of the room, wearing underwear, gone to the kitchen, pulled out a spoon from the drawer, and has taken the pot of soup and the spoon back with him into the room and closed the door.)

MAMA: I have always loved you. When you've been sick haven't I always wished it upon myself instead? Don't I give you the drumstick every time, Alix? Don't I bring you back candy when I can? Don't I hug you and smoothe your hair down enough? Any mother would beat you silly for what you're sayin' to me. Oh don't I give you money for stamps to send away for phoney certificates in the mail, Alix? Oh Damn why don't this door close? *(She throws her tissues at the door.)*

ALIX: That's a bona-fide certificate. It's more accomplishment than you ever had in your entire life.

MAMA: No, honey, there you are wrong, my biggest accomplishment was havin' my two children.

ALIX: *(angry again)* Sick! This is all makin' me sick. *(She whips around, goes to the door that Ray's behind and starts banging and kicking on it.)* I'm gonna bring her here. I don't care what you say. I'm gonna get Linda cause you stayin' in there is like the plague has fallen on this house. Black death has crept under the door, probably cause those gypsy holes in the porch, and it ain't your life anymore. It's mine and it's Mama's. *(She runs out of the house.)*

MAMA: Alix! Alix! You stay away from Garsha's. *(quiet voice.)* You hear, honey? *(She gets up, calms herself, walks out into the kitchen, starts wiping the flour off the counter.)* You know he said we were all gonna live in a house boat. We'd replenish the water in every other town. Kids would go swimmin' anytime they wanted, they'd get their schoolin' through the mail, you know he even sent away for those forms. But the main thing was we'd keep on movin', we wouldn't ever be stuck in one place and we'd catch fish like no tomorrow, he said. That was gonna be my second birthday gift.

THE PROMISE
by José Rivera
Patchogue, NY - Present - Lilia (18) - Lolin (39)

Lilia - A Puerto Rican girl who has lost her one true love
Lolin - Lila's neighborhood friend

Lilia is a young girl who has resingned herself to marrying the
rich yet odious man selected by her father. Her true love is
dead, killed by her father's mythological fighting rooster. Here,
her friend and neighbor, Lolin, tries to comfort her before the
wedding.

*(LILIA quickly throws the knife on the ground. LOLIN sees LILIA,
gasps—then laughs.)*
LOLIN: That's *you!* I'm standing here, going, "Guzman did it: He
brought his wife back from the dead!" *(Sniffs)* That's her perfume.
LILIA: *(Weak)* Papi's idea.
LOLIN: You look and smell like the friggin' past. *(Continues putting
up balloons and streamers)* It's nice you're wearing your mother's
dress. That's respect.
LILIA: It's cold.
LOLIN: You're nervous. I was the same way my first four times.
(Keeping one eye on LILIA, LOLIN finishes decorating the yard.) My
kids are in your house, eating. They ate a chair and two plates before
I stopped them. So if you want lunch, you better get some fast.
LILIA: I don't want lunch.
LOLIN: Why not? *(No answer. LILIA walks away.)* Do you think I
don't watch you? This is like two weeks without food for you, huh?
LILIA: *(Weakly)* What's new with you? Anything new...?
LOLIN: For Chrissakes Lilly, Carmelo is dead, that's all, that's it.
He's not in the armband. Or in this heavy air of yours full of poison—.
LILIA: Papi said you sold your house...?
*(LILIA walks away from LOLIN, trance-like, distant. She stares
forlornly into the pit.)*
LOLIN: Yeah. They started dumping some weird new chemical into
the pit and Tuesday I caught one of my kids eating a rock that was
glowing. I said, screw this, I'm getting out of this damn town.

THE PROMISE

LILIA: Where? Far?

LOLIN: Some place where I can find real men with *spines*...not the...backbones of sugar water and mother's milk holding up the "men" of Patchogue.

LILIA: I hope, when you find your new man, you two will visit me. I hope...in the middle of Muñoz's money...the rooms of our big house...the teeth of our children...I hope you can still find me...

(LILIA turns away, fighting tears of anger.)

LOLIN: Lilly, if you don't want to go through with the wedding, don't. Please. But decide now. A pig's gonna be killed for you—.

LILIA: *(Sad laugh)* I decided to marry Mr. Muñoz a long time ago. It doesn't bother me.

LOLIN: Hey, maybe he won't be so bad. Huh? He wants you to go to college; he's rich; he's kinda cute. And maybe Carmelo wasn't the—.

LILIA: Please don't talk about him.

LOLIN: The truth: Carmelo burned a hole in your heart the size of God, right? And you're ready to fall in that hole and starve to death like...

LILIA: *Dammit, this dress is freezing—!*

(LILIA tears at her wedding dress, ripping pieces from it and throwing them around the yard. She is doing everything she can to fight her tears.)

(Beat. She calms down, realizing that fighting back is useless.)

LILIA: Sometimes, Lolly, I think I can still hear all the things he ever said to me: all his plans, his ideas. I can see the four children we wanted to have. Do you know where those things went after he died? *(LILIA touches her chest and stomach.)* I do. They're here. I'm saving them inside me. They're waiting for something good to happen in this goddamn world...something truly good...before they come back to be born. *(She looks at LOLIN, excited.)* I have to go to the cemetery. Come with me?

LOLIN: Now? The wedding's in an hour—.

LILIA: I want to invite him to the wedding.

LOLIN: Lilly! That's bad luck—.

LILIA: Don't be afraid. I know a short cut, c'mon.

164

THE REAL QUEEN OF HEARTS AIN'T EVEN PRETTY
by Brad Bailey
Girl's locker room - 1976 - Liz (18) - Cass (18)

Liz Nichols - Bright, funny and attractive
Cass Wilson - Liz's friend, average looks, a follower

Liz and Cass are best friends who have volunteered to watch over the personal possessions of the contestants during the Queen of Hearts Beauty Pagent. The two girls banter back and forth, revealing their thoughts on the contest, their school and the future.

LIZ: *(applying the lipstick)* ...And nobody could believe it when she won Queen of Hearts that year.
CASS: What year?
LIZ: The year Connie and them graduated. 1969. Yeah, Sharon Porter was Queen of Hearts in '69.
CASS: I heard it was just a joke.
LIZ: No, It was real!
CASS: But Sharon Porter?
LIZ: Yeah. *(Takes the lipstick from her lips.)* Everybody used to call her Sharon Pooter. *(Makes a flatulent noise with her newly-painted lips.)*
CASS: *(Laughs.)* God. What kinda judges did they *have* back then?
LIZ: Weren't any judges. I mean, there were judges, but not like out there. *(Indicates offstage right.)* Back then, the contest wasn't a beauty walk or anything like now.
CASS: Surely to God she wasn't elected.
LIZ: Naw. It was because of her class picture.
CASS: You're kidding.
LIZ: Nope. They got all the girls in the school to submit a picture and then sent 'em off somewhere to be judged.
CASS: Who by?
LIZ: That year it was some people at Southern Living Magazine. They just picked the girl that looked the best in her picture.
CASS: *Sharon Porter?*

THE REAL QUEEN OF HEARTS AIN'T EVEN PRETTY

LIZ: I don't know how, but her picture was beautiful. I mean it. They took it through a smudged lens or something.

CASS: *Real* smudged.

LIZ: It looked real glamorous—like a movie star or something.

CASS: Southern Living Magazine?

LIZ: Yep.

CASS: What do they know about a beauty contest?

LIZ: I saw in a old yearbook where one time they sent the pictures out to Hollywood to be judged.

CASS: *(dreamily)* Hollywood.

LIZ: That year, Queen of Hearts was picked by-are your ready? Tiny Tim and Miss Vicki.

CASS: God.

LIZ: *Tiny Tim and Miss Vicki!* And then one year, they sent all the pictures down to Montgomery and the Young Democrats picked the winner.

CASS: Who'd they pick?

LIZ: *(Laughs.)* Rita Woods.

CASS: Rita Woods!

LIZ: *(offhand.)* Yeah. Everybody said she won just becasue she looked so much like George Wallace. Except for the mustache.

CASS: He hasn't got a mustache.

LIZ: I was talking about *Rita*.

CASS: *(laughing)* You're crazy!

LIZ: *(grandly)* And that's the reason for all this mess. Because you can't judge beauty from pictures. So they decided to make it a beautywalk.

CASS: *(pointing to lipstick)* Whose is that?

LIZ: Nancy Noblett's. *(turning from mirror to face CASS)* What do you think?

CASS: Umm. I don't know.

LIZ: I think it's too much.

CASS: Yeah. Too much. *(Points to an elaborate evening gown hanging prominently nearby.)* Who's wearing this?

LIZ: Nobody. It's Sherri Lee's. She decided to wear something else.

THE REAL QUEEN OF HEARTS AIN'T EVEN PRETTY

CASS: Again?

LIZ: Yeah. Again. *(Beat)* After I already spit on it and everything. *(CASS laughs again.)* I really wanted to kill her last night.

CASS: When?

LIZ: *(crossing to CASS)* At rehearsal last night. Well, her old mother, too. Dragging in six suits for streetwear and four gowns. *(She jumps up on the bench and mimicks.)* "I want to see which one looks the best under the lights. Sherri Lee has such delicate coloring and all, I want to pick just the right shade"— *(dropping her pose)* Shit. I just can't believe Sherri Lee's in this contest.

CASS: Everybody hates her guts.

LIZ: The boys don't. They think she's something great. I thought it was kinda funny when all the clubs elected girls to be in Queen of Hearts. Sherri Lee was nominated in every club—by the *boys*—but the *girls* always voted her out. Beta Club, F.T.A., Library Club, same thing. The boys would nominate her and the girls would vote for *anybody* else but Sherri Lee.

CASS: *(matter-of-factly)* Well she's in the contest.

LIZ: We ran out of girls!

CASS: You got nominated. You turned it down.

LIZ: Last year was enough for me. Anyway, no girls were left and Sherri Lee *had* to get in. But she was the last one. How do you think Diane Batson got in? *(With her arms she indicates DIANE's size.)*

CASS: God.

LIZ: I mean, I like Diane and all, but she's no beauty. She's so fat, she can't get school insurance to cover her.

CASS: Really?

LIZ: And in P.E., they won't let her get *near* the trampoline. Everybody else is jumping up and down on the trampoline and there's Diane, way over yonder, jumping on a wrestling mat.

CASS: God, Liz.

LIZ: Yeah, we did a real good job of keeping Sherri Lee out of the contest—us girls did.

CASS: Until Ag Class.

LIZ: Those stupid-ass boys. I could kill 'em every one.

THE REAL QUEEN OF HEARTS AIN'T EVEN PRETTY

CASS: I know it.

LIZ: They think Sherri Lee's such a sweet little thing. Just because she's the new girl in school. You know how she acts around boys.

CASS: Stupid-ass boys.

LIZ: She's a damned goody-goody. Miss Head Majorette—Miss Feature Twirler. And she's engaged. Or she says she is. Why do the boys like her? She's getting married.

CASS: She's such a goody-goody.

LIZ: Can't you just hear her in her interview tonight? I bet she really slobbered all over those judges. *(mimicking)* "My names' Sherri Lee Speer, and I'm representing the Future Farmers of America. My hobbies are sign language, reading to shut-ins, and praying a lot. In my spare time, I'm a volunteer seeing-eye person for blind dogs."

CASS: *(howling)* You're crazy!

LIZ: All I can say is, she's in pretty bad shape when she's the last girl in the whole school to get picked for Queen of Hearts.

CASS: *(seriously)* I didn't get picked.

LIZ: Well, yeah...but...you didn't want to, remember? I asked you to help me back here. You didn't wanna be in this shitty contest.

CASS: Yes, I did.

LIZ: No, you didn't.

CASS: I kinda did.

LIZ: You're not missing a thing.

CASS: You were in it last year.

LIZ: Big deal.

CASS: First alternate.

LIZ: Big deal.

CASS: It *is* a big deal. You could've won it too—if you'da tried. *(LIZ laughs.)* Well, you *could've*. But no, you go out there in evening wear chewing on a wad of gum as big as my fist.

LIZ: *(Laughs.)* I forgot to spit it out.

CASS: You did not. You did it on purpose.

LIZ: *(grinning)* No, I didn't.

CASS: Liz, you blew a bubble a foot wide.

LIZ: *(mock-indignation)* I did not.

168

THE REAL QUEEN OF HEARTS AIN'T EVEN PRETTY

CASS: There's a picture in the yearbook.

LIZ: Oh, yeah.

CASS: "Oh yeah"—and you coulda *won* it too, Liz, if—

LIZ: God, Cass, you act like it's the damned Miss America Pagent or something. It's no big deal.

CASS: It is *here*.

LIZ: My God, yes! Such an honor! They throw a dozen half-dead roses in your hands and stick a tacky little crown on your head and push you out front, and you walk around the gym and people clap and yell and whistle—and old men squint at your tits—and you smile, but just a little, or your gums'll show in all the pictures—and you cry, but just a little, or your mascara'll run, and all the time, Eddie Akers is singing into a microphone: *(She strikes a hammy pose and sings.)* "So meet the lovely Queen of Hearts..."

CASS: *(laughing)* He's such a queer.

LIZ: Who's a queer?

CASS: Eddie Akers.

LIZ: He is not.

CASS: *(proof positive)* Liz, he wears an I.D. *bracelet*.

LIZ: So what?

CASS: And he's always messing with the girls' hair.

LIZ: Cass, if he was a queer, he's be messing with the *boys'* hair.

CASS: Well, maybe he does.

LIZ: He does not. And he's *not* a queer.

CASS: *(walking away)* Well, if I'd known you were in *love* with Eddie Akers, I never woulda mentioned it.

LIZ: I'm not in *love* with Eddie Akers.

CASS: He's always hanging around you. He's in love with you. I think he's sickening.

LIZ: *(enjoying this)* You're jealous. You're jealous, but who of? Me or Eddie?

CASS: I'm not jealous! I just hate him, that's all.

LIZ: *(craftily)* He likes you.

CASS: Bull.

LIZ: He drew that picture of you.

THE REAL QUEEN OF HEARTS AIN'T EVEN PRETTY

CASS: I know it.

LIZ: And he had it framed, too.

CASS: I know it.

LIZ: He has a crush on you.

CASS: *God.*

LIZ: He's kinda cute too. I think. Don't you think he's cute?

CASS: Cute?

LIZ: Yeah. Yeah, I think he's cute. Don't you think he's cute?

CASS: Well, I guess—in an ugly sort of way.

LIZ: Would you go to the prom with him?

CASS: NO WAY! *(then hopefully)* Do you think maybe he might ask me?

LIZ: He'll ask you.

CASS: How do you know?

LIZ: I just know.

CASS: *(suspiciously)* Did you tell Eddie Akers to ask me?

LIZ: No, I *paid* him to ask you!

CASS: LIZ!

LIZ: Not really.

CASS: Did he tell you to ask me?

LIZ: No.

CASS: Then why did you say that?

LIZ: *(candidly)* Do you have a date for the prom?

CASS: Do *you*?

LIZ: Yes.

CASS: You didn't tell me. Who with?

LIZ: Greg.

CASS: Greg Atkins?

LIZ: Yeah.

CASS: *Why?*

LIZ: Why not.

CASS: But Tony asked you. And Rob did, too.

LIZ: Football players.

CASS: So?

LIZ: I don't date football players.

CASS: *You're* head cheerleader.

LIZ: And everybody knows cheerleaders date football players. Well, I don't.

CASS: But Greg Atkins?

LIZ: Greg's a genius. He's gonna be Valedictorian and everything.

CASS: But nobody likes him.

LIZ: I do.

CASS: But he doesn't play football or anything.

LIZ: That's right, Cass. And because he doesn't have a neck like a tree trunk and sweat like a pig, the hicks here don't like him.

CASS: *I* don't like him.

LIZ: Well, you're not going to the prom with him, either.

CASS: And I wouldn't either.

LIZ: You'd go with anybody that'd ask you.

CASS: I would not.

LIZ: You sure are picky for somebody who doesn't have a date. You don't have a date do you?

CASS: Why do you think I don't?

LIZ: 'Cause if you did, youda written his name all over your notebooks.

CASS: Well.

LIZ: *(enthusiastically)* I told Eddie Akers to ask you.

CASS: *(walking away)* No thanks.

LIZ: Why not?

CASS: I don't want a date.

LIZ: You're not going to our Senior Prom?

CASS: I'm going. I just don't want a date.

LIZ: *Everybody* wants a date.

CASS: *(resentfully)* You've changed *your* mind.

LIZ: Changed my mind?

CASS: About the prom. Us going together.

LIZ: Oh.

CASS: It's what you said.

LIZ: Cass...

CASS: You *said*. You said we'd go together—just me and you—we'd get drunk as hell and go to the prom.

LIZ: *(ashamed)* I know.

CASS: But that was before *you* had a date.

LIZ: Cass.

CASS: It doesn't matter. I don't care.

LIZ: You're mad. *(Beat)* Cass, we'll see each other there—at the prom. *(Silence. LIZ crosses the table, gets brush and hesitantly begins to brush CASS's ponytail. She tries to lighten the mood.)* Hey. Did you see how drunk Debbie was? Huh?

CASS: *(Mumbles.)* Yeah.

LIZ: She's really drunk. I had to do her make-up for her. She kept poking herself in the eyeball with the mascara. *(This gets a stifled smile from CASS.)* Hey. They drank four bottles of Boone's Farm.

CASS: *(succumbing to LIZ's charm)* What kind?

LIZ: Strawberry Hill.

CASS: Who?

LIZ: Her and Sara.

CASS: God.

LIZ: Last year, I was so drunk, I couldn't see.

CASS: Really?

LIZ: Uh huh. And Phyllis and them had some pot.

CASS: *(shocked)* Pot? *Marijuana?*

LIZ: Yeah.

CASS: Here at school?

LIZ: Yeah.

CASS: You couldn't tell.

LIZ: Tell what?

CASS: That you were drunk or—*stoned*. You acted normal. Except for when you blew the bubble. You couldn't tell.

LIZ: *I* could tell. *(still brushing)* Hey. You know Cindy.

CASS: Yeah.

LIZ: Last year Cindy smoked some dope right before she had to go down for her interview with the judges.

CASS: What happened?

LIZ: She disappeared! Nobody could find her and the judges were calling her number.

CASS: God.

LIZ: People were looking for here everywhere. I finally found her. Up in the bandroom.

CASS: In the bandroom?

LIZ: Behind the sousaphone. She was a mess.

CASS: What did you do?

LIZ: Walked her around a little and then sent her on down to the judges.

CASS: She went to the interview? Like that?

LIZ: *(matter-of-factly)* That's the whole *point* of the thing, Cass.

CASS: What?

LIZ: To see how messed up you can get and still *do it*—be in the contest.

CASS: Oh.

LIZ: Those interviews are so stupid, anyway. They ask you things like "Why do you want to be Queen of Hearts?" and "If you had one wish, what would it be?"

CASS: God. How stupid.

LIZ: Yeah. And Cindy gets in there *somehow* and sits down in front of the judges. And some old lady judge with like, blue hair and cat-eye classes, looks at Cindy and says— *(a nasal voice)* "Tell us, Miss, about your hobbies." And Cindy leans over the table and goes— *(Theme music for "The Twilight Zone.")*
Do do do do,
Do do do do... *(They both laugh loudly.)*

CASS: *(still laughing)* Hey, Liz?

LIZ: *(laughing)* Huh?

CASS: I don't get it.

LIZ: Neither do I, but it was great! *(laughing)* And Cindy still got in the top ten!

CASS: Is anybody messed up tonight?

LIZ: Not like that. Well, I don't know. I was too busy trying to get 'em ready. *(She looks as SHERRI LEE's gown.)* You know what?

CASS: What?

173

THE REAL QUEEN OF HEARTS AIN'T EVEN PRETTY

LIZ: I'd love to see Sherri Lee stoned.

CASS: Yeah. That would be fun. *(Beat. Then CASS sings.)*
Do do do do,
Do do do do... *(CASS laughs. LIZ stares at the gown.)*

LIZ: You think she'll win?

CASS: Do you?

LIZ: She's got a good chance.

CASS: Donna might win.

LIZ: Yeah, Donna's pretty, but did you see her *dress?*

CASS: Yeah.

LIZ: That's about the ugliest dress I've ever seen on a human. Looked like it was made by Helen Keller.

CASS: Donna said *she* made it.

LIZ: I know, but she shouldn't admit it. She ought to say her mother made it.

CASS: She thought it would impress the judges if they knew she made it herself.

LIZ: It will—if she walks out there with a German Shepherd and a white cane.

SALLY AND MARSHA
by Sybille Pearson
NYC apartment - Present - Sally (30's) - Marsha (30's)

Sally - A gal from the country living in the city
Marsha - Sally's neighbor, a New Yorker

Sally and Marsha are two very differnt women drawn together
by a mutual need for companionship. Wholesome, countrybred
Sally helps neurotic Marsha to get her life back under control.
In turn, Marsha does her best to introduce Sally to city life.
Here, the two share a moment of revelation.

*(Sally is seated on couch, making peanut puppets. The coffee table is
covered with a tray containing yarn, beads, glue, etc., and an open
scrapbook. Marsha has a new short hairdo; her sweater is blue. She
is happy and restless, sits in the rocker, and attempts to juggle peanuts;
most of them fall on the floor.)*

SALLY: Come sit next to me.

MARSHA: What about a movie? Where's the *Times*? *(She jumps up.)*

SALLY: I thought you were buying it.

MARSHA: Forgot.

MARSHA: Shit. No, not shit. There's always a theater in the Village
that has Bertolucci. You like him?

SALLY: Don't know him.

MARSHA: That's it! *(She gets Sally's coat out of the closet.)* First,
we're going to Rienzi's, have a fat cappucino, then there's a hero place
on...

SALLY: It's almost noon.

MARSHA: *(Tosses coat to Sally.)* So I'll tell the cab driver you're
having the baby. We'll get meat-ball heroes with five napkins, eat them
in the movies, get a cab back and you'll be here by three.

SALLY: I don't feel like a movie.

MARSHA: Why not!

SALLY: I got a headache.

MARSHA: I'll buy you an aspirin hero.

SALLY: Not today... Come. Sit quiet next to me and make a peanut

175

puppet. *(Marsha grabs a handful of peanuts and walks to rocker. She stops midway and freezes.)*
MARSHA: I hear it. My mother's packing her little broomstick. *(She bends her ear to stomach.)* Tell me. When will mother arrive? Eight days! Mother and Thanksgiving will be here in eight days. *(Sally gets up and goes to kitchen.)*
SALLY: You're losing your marbles. *(Marsha flops in rocker, shells peanuts on floor, and eats them.)*
MARSHA: You see, the Japanese think the soul resides in the stomach, but I know that tucked under the pancreas, undetectable by x-rays, there's a clock that tells people when their mother is coming to visit. And exactly eight days before her arrival, it sends up a message of uncontrollable hunger. *(Sally sticks a Saltine in Marsha's mouth.)*
SALLY: Whistle Yankee Doodle. *(Sally returns to couch and her scrapbook and puppet. Marsha attempts whistling and inadvertently spits all over scrapbook.)* Damn you're a kletz!
MARSHA: Klutz. *(She cleans off page of scrapbook.)* I'm sorry.
SALLY: Didn't mean to yell.
MARSHA: *(Flipping through scrapbook.)* Painting with lard! *(She takes book to rocker.)* Whose is this? How to make hats or bird feather out of bleach bottles.
SALLY: Can I have it back?
MARSHA: Who devoted their life to this?
SALLY: It's a friend's.
MARSHA: I bet you it's Joni's. Joyful Joni. The one who opened the champagne to let it breathe.
SALLY: I never told you that.
MARSHA: She lockes herself in the bathroom and reads "Heloise's Household Tips," and I bet you her fucking pineapple upside down cake that I'm right.
SALLY: What she just got a is twenty-three caret gold Oneida table setting, a twelve-hundred-dollar modular sofa, AND, any day now, Rusty's going to buy her a motel.
MARSHA: A motel?
SALLY: Going to give it her name. Going to be under Mt. Rushmore.

SALLY AND MARSHA

MARSHA: That's obscene. *(She jumps up.)* Let's go out. Let's have lobsters!

SALLY: I got tuna in the fridge.

MARSHA: Is it that you're ashamed to go out with me now that I'm so beautiful?

SALLY: *(Excited.)* You didn't tell me? Did Martin like your hair?

MARSHA: He said I looked less Chekovian.

SALLY: That mean he liked what I did?

MARSHA: You haven't read Chekov!

SALLY: No.

MARSHA: *(Running to bookcase.)* Where's the list? He's got to go on the list. *(She finds list and pencil and writes.)* Did you finish "Little Dorrit"?

SALLY: No.

MARSHA: *(Writing.)* Finish it, and then we'll do Fielding before we hit Austen. And the entire Bronte family including Branwell. *(She tosses paper aside and goes to Sally.)* We're going. We're going to the Strand. Twenty dollars can get you twenty, forty books. We'll take a cab down. I'll take my cab from there to Heintz. You'll take your cab...

SALLY: I can't.

MARSHA: Yes. You can.

SALLY: Why can't you just sit down next to me!

MARSHA: Anybody can do that.

SALLY: Then make a puppet with me! I promised the kids a puppet show the first rainy afternoon.

MARSHA: All children should go to boarding school, then there wouldn't be anything like afternoons.

SALLY: You couldn't live without afternoons. You see your doctor every one... Look at this mess. *(Sally gets up and picks peanut shells from the floor.)*

MARSHA: I was going to do it. *(She gets ash tray and helps pick up shells.)* I'll pay you for them.

SALLY: *(Picking up shells.)* Don't ever talk about paying me. Besides, you've given me too many things already.

SALLY AND MARSHA

MARSHA: I only gave you what I didn't need.

SALLY: You're going to want your blender back.

MARSHA: I can't stand appliances.

SALLY: *(Finding peanuts under couch.)* Sure gota lot of things you can't stand.

MARSHA: I didn't buy them.

SALLY: Still got them.

MARSHA: Men give you appliances to take away your right to complain. *(Marsha starts to kitchen with shells.)*

SALLY: I'll do it.

MARSHA: I can carry them into the kitchen.

SALLY: I'll do it! *(Sally brings ash tray to kitchen.)*

MARSHA: *I'll* do the living room. *(She takes tray of puppet materials and a book that's lying on the coffee table and brings them to bookcase.)* How can you have this in your house where the kids can see it?

SALLY: *(Returning.)* What?

MARSHA: Dale Carnegie.

SALLY: *(Entering)* That man is like part of our family.

MARSHA: Burn it! This asshole is responsible for more frozen smiles than Birdseye. *(Sally takes book from Marsha, sits on couch and reads, aloud, to herself.)* I'll race you for a bagel and lox. *(Sally doesn't respond.)* I'm sorry... *(Marsha nudges Sally.)* Hey, I said I'm sorry.

SALLY: I am reading. Can't you see I am reading.

MARSHA: I see that.

SALLY: You read when I talk to you. I read when you talk to me.

MARSHA: What are you cracking up for?

SALLY: On your way *out* take "Little Dorrit" with you. It's boring and the pages fall out when you turn it.

MARSHA: Fine. *(She picks up scrapbook.)* Why don't you read this shit, too. *(Sally pulls book out of her hands.)*

SALLY: That's mine! I made it. *(The cover tears.)* Look what you did.

MARSHA: I didn't do a thing. You pulled it.

SALLY: *(Trying to fix cover.)* What you have to touch it for?

178

SALLY AND MARSHA

MARSHA: Why didn't you tell me it was yours?

SALLY: And have to sit through a five-hour lecture on art? You can't even knit a pot holder.

MARSHA: I'm proud of that.

SALLY: Cause you're a blank on imagination.

MARSHA: All I have is imagination!

SALLY: All you have is opinions.

MARSHA: Because I don't have orgasms over blenders? *(Sally heads for the kitchen to get blender.)*

SALLY: You're taking it back.

MARSHA: *(Following.)* I'll put it in the incinerator. *(Sally, with blender in hand, stops in archway and blocks Marsha's entry to kitchen.)*

SALLY: Don't come in my kitchen!

MARSHA: Why am I never allowed...

SALLY: And you'll never be. I'm giving your blender to the church and going to get my own when Ted gets his first Cousin.

MARSHA: I was in the best mood I was ever in in my life this morning! I wanted to go out. When in my life have I ever wanted to go out and all you could relate to was putting wigs on peanuts!

SALLY: *(Irrationally angry.)* Where do I live?

MARSHA: Here.

SALLY: How many rooms I got?

MARSHA: Two and a half.

SALLY: Do I sleep in a fold-up bed?

MARSHA: *(Beginning to be exasperated.)* Yes.

SALLY: Do I have a vacuum of my own?

MARSHA: No.

SALLY: Do I have a TV, dishwasher, dryer, orange juice squeezer?

MARSHA: No. No. No. No.

SALLY: Where do you live?

MARSHA: *(Starting to shout.)* There.

SALLY: How many rooms you got?

MARSHA: Eight.

SALLY: Why can't I go out with you?

SALLY AND MARSHA

MARSHA: *(Shouting louder.)* Why the fuck can't you go out with me?

SALLY: *(Shouting louder.)* Because I don't have the money.

MARSHA: *(Shouting louder.)* I would have given it to you.

SALLY: I don't take charity!

MARSHA: I'm shouting!

SALLY: YES.

MARSHA: I've never shouted at another woman before.

SALLY: *(Still shouting.)* Me neither.

MARSHA: You didn't shout at Joni?

SALLY: NO.

MARSHA: *(Shouting)* I'm the first woman you ever shouted at?

SALLY: YES.

MARSHA: Thank you...thank you.

SALLY: I got to get some O.J.

MARSHA: Don't move. I want to get it for you. I'm going to serve you.

SALLY: *(Softly.)* I don't want you to go in there.

MARSHA: Why?

SALLY: *(With difficulty.)* The place is crawling with roaches.

MARSHA: Everybody in New York has roaches. Even Greta Garbo and she's Nordic.

SALLY: I'd like very much for you to get me an orange juice.

(Sally sits on couch. Marsha goes in kitchen.)

MARSHA: I feel like Richard Burton going to Mecca.

SALLY: What picture was that?

MARSHA: Different Burton. *(She gets juice out of ice box.)* Sir Richard. He was a nineteenth-century explorer... You too must die. *(She slams spatula on roach. She enters living room and speaks excitedly as she finishes Sally's glass of juice.)* You are going to flip over Burton. Not only was he the first white man to go to Mecca, but he discovered Lake Tanganyika, translated the Arabian Nights which is part pure erotica, spoke twenty-eight languages, AND married Isabel Arrundel who was as exciting as he... *(She sees Sally's expression.)* Shit, I'll never change. I'm a twentieth-century neurotic and a lecturing bore.

SALLY AND MARSHA

SALLY: I agree.

MARSHA: You're not supposed to agree.

SALLY: No? Whose orange juice was that?

MARSHA: Yours. *(She goes to kitchen quickly to get more juice.)* You're so fucking good, good, good, and I'm a shit.

SALLY: H. I'm not so great. *(Marsha re-enters with juice.)* I'm turning ugly, Mash...I'm a shit.

MARSHA: Sally.

SALLY: I'm a jealous woman.

MARSHA: Who? Of me?

SALLY: You, Joni, people in the subway. Anybody that's got things.

MARSHA: I've got things and look at me. Money's not...

SALLY: I know money's not happiness. I was bred on that.

MARSHA: You don't need things.

SALLY: I thought that. It was easy. I'd flip through magazines, look at a nice set of china. But if you only see a picture, it looks like a dream. And if it's not meant, you close the page and go on with your life. But here. God, when I took the kids to ride the escalators at Macy's, nothing seemed like a dream. I could touch everything. Watch people picking things out, carrying things out. I don't even know what's in the packages, but I sit in the subways now guessing what's in them and *wanting* it. I can't close that store out of my mind. And Ted comes home after twelve hours of killing himself, bringing home nothing. And I'm wanting things. I can't tell him that. Unless I walk blind in this city, I don't know how I'm going to shake it. I want to wake up tomorrow morning and be a hundred thousand-dollar wife. *I want it...* You haven't heard anything uglier than that, have you?

MARSHA: *(After a beat between them.)* I don't think you're ugly. *(After a moment of silence, Marsha sits next to Sally on the couch.)*

SALLY: It's nice. Sitting quiet next to a gal. It's nice.

MARSHA: You do that with Joni?

SALLY: She wasn't a friend.

MARSHA: You said she was your best friend.

SALLY: *(Smiling.)* I know what I said. *(The two women sit quietly as the lights dim.)*

THE SECRET SITS IN THE MIDDLE
by Lisa Marie Radano
Coney Island - Present - Tina (20's) - Angela (20's-30's)

Tina - A young woman seeking an abortion
Angela - Tina's sister

Tina has asked her sister, Angela, to take her to the clinic for a
pregnancy test. Here, Tina returns to the waiting room after
finding out that she is, in fact, pregnant.

*(ANGELA POMPEII, a young woman, casually dressed, sits waiting in
a drab waiting room. There are no pictures on the walls. There is a
drab couch with low end tables at either end. There are also some drab
and uncomfortable chairs with additional matching end tables. Upstage
right is a door. This door bursts open and through it comes TINA
POMPEII, ANGELA's younger sister. She has teased, moussed,
sprayed hair, pastel face makeup, very tight pastel stretch jeans, pastel
hightop leather sneakers with matching socks, pastel top, accessories,
and jewelry.)*

ANGELA: Well? What did they say?

TINA: *(Prowling around the waiting room)* I'm knocked up. Jesus!
Where's the magazines? I can't believe it! Not-a single solitary
magazine in the whold stinky place. It's like too much ta believe. A
waiting room and NO magazines!

ANGELA: That's it?

TINA: What Angela, what. Don't look at me like you just stepped in
something.

ANGELA: That's it— I'm knocked up—where's the magazines?
What is that? That is NOT the reaction of a human being.

TINA: Yea well after everything I just been through, I'm not feelen
too much like-a human being. I mean, whatya think I been doin in
there the past hour? Soaken in perfumed milk? NO! I been peeing
into multiple cups—tryen to lie still while I had what felt like four setsa
hands shoven up inside-a me and punchen me down like-a pizza dough,
meanwhile some smarmy male nurse from Bombay, you know, a dot-
head, comes in ta give my tits one final check just ta make sure, of

182

what I don't know, that I got 'em maybe. I swear, they got-a buncha totally tweaked out people back there! ONE HOUR! One hour it took them ta tell me, "Miss Pompeii, you are pregnant." Well rope me up and call me doggie, I say. Tell me something I don't know, now let's alter this situation, like pronto. "Well Miss Pompeii, first you must wait in the waiting room. We believe in giving every woman some time to ruminate before taking this weighty step." Never take the steps if there is an escalator I say. But no. I gotta come out here and ponder about very sad kinduv save the whale things. You know, MUCHO sad consequence kindsa things. And looken around me I can see the decor- a this room is just right for sufferen. So do me a favor and no speeches please. I just wish I could look at some color photos and pretend I'm in one of 'em.

ANGELA: Well how can I serve you? Maybe there's a nice civilized dentist office somewhere in the building. I could run and borrow a National Geographic so you could look at pictures of penguins and people with plates in their lips.

TINA: Angela. Huh uh. You're maken me unhappy I brought you with me.

ANGELA: You should get down on your hands and knees and crawl across this crummy carpet in thanks-ta me for comen!

TINA: You're right. I am sorry. THANKS for comen.

ANGELA: Don't be a fucken dope—I'm your sister. Who else?

TINA: Let's just sit down, and wait.

(They both settle into the couch, arranging themselves.)

TINA: Could I have my candy bar...please?

(Angela takes from her puse, a Milky Way bar, and hands it to Tina. Tina rips it open like a cannibal rips open a throat. Savagely. She shoves huge bites into her mouth chewing with her eyes closed making eating noises.)

ANGELA: Easy kid.

TINA: I can't help it. OHHHHH. I feel much better now. I don't know what it is, unless I got chocolate in my mouth, I feel like sobbing.

ANGELA: You're pregnant. Your hormones are cryen out for cocoa products.

TINA: Please. Don't ruin it for me. I just spent fifteen minutes with

THE SECRET SITS IN THE MIDDLE

some Nordic dyke in coveralls who showed me charts of the female gen-i-tal-i-a. A POINTING STICK she used, ta point out glands and eggs and fellow-pia tubing, and between you and me, the whole damn works is dog ugly. It's a lucky thing we wear clothes. Did we get me two Milky Ways?

ANGELA: NO. You said you wanted a Kit Kat for crispiness.

TINA: What was I thinken.

ANGELA: WELL. How far along are you?

TINA: I dunno. Four weeks, five maybe. I forget. Jeez. I could REALLY go for a slice and big can-a Yoo Hoo. Now I know why Aunt Nina's such a fat cow.

ANGELA: Aunt Nina ain't no fat cow! She's a solid woman, yes. But just because she's had six kids is no reason to talk like Motherhood is a disfigurin event.

TINA: Oh get out Angela. Aunt Nina gotta buy her bras in The Big And Tall Shop. You could carpet a bathroom wida pair-a her slacks.

ANGELA: I don't see why you gotta lash out by saying evil things about family. But if this is the first step on the road to you actually sayen something FEELING about this situation, then gahead and get alla your filthy poison out on me. That's why I'm here.

TINA: No Angela, see the truth is—the only reason I asked you to come is because I don't think I'll wanna drive when this is over with which I HOPE IS SOON! Now—could I have me Kit Kat...please?

ANGELA: *(Throwing the candy bar in the direction of Tina's head)* HERE! Here's your Kit Kat Miss Hoover Upright! Eat it and be surly! I hope you get an inverted pimple!

TINA: I already did! Can you see it!?

ANGELA: No. I can not.

TINA: Well. That's because I'm a genius wit make-up.

ANGELA: Speaken of which—don't you think you're a little overdressed for the occasion? This ain't no Star Search ya know.

TINA: It's important ta me ta look my best.

ANGELA: You got some set-a values on you. On a day like today, alls you care about is how you BUTT looks in jeans. You're like beguiled by it. I see you trying to check it out in car fenders and bank windows.

THE SECRET SITS IN THE MIDDLE

TINA: Are you callen me self absorbed?

ANGELA: No. I'M self absorbed. YOU'RE vain and stupid.

TINA: Well at least I don't dress like I'm just taken out the garbage. Maybe that's how come I gotta boyfriend.

ANGELA: Oh yea... So where IS Mr. Humpen High this morning?

TINA: He hadda work.

ANGELA: He hadda work.

TINA: Yea he hadda work.

ANGELA: He hadda. He couldn't get his Father to watch that crummy carwash for one morning outa your lives?

TINA: It is NOT crummy! It's the largest and most successful carwash in alla Brooklyn. They use well water! The estimated worth is two million and Sonny stands to inherit.

ANGELA: I hate that carwash. It's like a southern plantation and Sonny is nothen morena slave driver. Him and his whole family. The way they treat those black guys is sickening.

TINA: Those men are no good drunks. Sonny gives em something useful ta do. If it weren't for Sonny and the carwash, they'd probably be out knifen people at gunpoint.

ANGELA: Whoa. Sonny ain't no arch angel. He's parta the problem. The way it works at the carwash is like a starving rat eating it's own foot and then growen back a new one. At the enda the day Sonny pays the men their lousy minimum wage—in cash—which they take across the street to the liquor store. Sonny should just pay em in Thunderbird. The next morning they figure, if they're gonna get the brown bag at the enda the day, they gotta go first to Sonny. So you see? He owns their hides. And it never stops. The rat just keeps growen more feet.

TINA: You know. When you talk like that your face get's all scrunched up and your nose sortuv hooks under. It's not a great look for you and I'll bet it makes guys run away at top speed. Maybe that's how come I gotta boyfriend. I don't go around maken speeches which scrunch up my face. MY face is for other things.

ANGELA: Like PUNCHEN!

TINA: No. My face is for Sonny to hold in his two hands and kiss.

ANGELA: Then why is it that you and your face are sitten here with me insteada him?

SO WHEN YOU GET MARRIED...
by Ellen Byron
Brooklyn - Present - Louisa (50's) - Mimi (31)

Louisa DiVangilito Hartfeld - Bright but filled with nervous
    energy. The much-loved black
    sheep of the family
Mimi Hartfeld - Louisa's daughter. Sensitive and artistic

A family wedding serves to bring out the worst between mother
and daughter as an argument commences between the two in the
powder room of the catering hall.

LOUISA: Mimi, Mimi, they're gonna throw the bouquet. Billy said
they'd keep up the drumroll 'til you got out there.
MIMI: YOU—I'm not even talking to you after sicking
that...that...CREEP on me—
LOUISA: Everytime I try to help—
MIMI: "HELP"!
LOUISA: Okay, okay, forget Billy, forget the cadet, forget everything
I said—do it for the *family*. Everyone's dying for you to catch the
bouquet.
MIMI: I absolutely refuse. I'm not letting you or the family control
my life anymore. I have had *e-nough.*
LOUISA: I never controlled your life.
MIMI: Are you kidding? You've never stopped. Every since I was
little.
LOUISA: How? Tell me, please, I'd love to know how I committed
these great crimes I know nothing about.
MIMI: I could give you a million examples.
LOUISA: Okay, fine, go ahead.
MIMI: Okay, fine, I will. Remember the Mary Janes?
LOUISA: The what?
MIMI: Remember when I was in kindergarten you made me wear
those stupid Mary Jane shoes, the ones that couldn't be closed without
that awful button hook?
LOUISA: What are you talking about? I bought those shoes because

186

they looked cute on you. What does that have to do with controlling your life?

MIMI: *Aha*, they looked cute, but if they ever came undone, I'd spend the rest of the day with my shoes flapping on and off and the teacher making comments about why I didn't wear saddleshoes like everyone else. They could never be buttoned because YOU had the hook.

LOUISA: You should have told me, I would have given your teacher a spare hook.

MIMI: I am talking about what the shoes represent, the symbolism.

LOUISA: What symbolism? I just thought they were cute.

MIMI: No, you were controlling me.

LOUISA: You were six years old—

MIMI: So?

LOUISA: I was only trying to do what I thought was best for you.

MIMI: Famous last words.

LOUSIA: This is the most ridiculous conversation I've ever had. *(She begins to leave.)*

MIMI: Mother, wait—if you really want to do what's best for me, please, PLEASE, ask Noona to give me my dowry so I can have a place to live and work.

LOUISA: Why should I?

MIMI: Why should you?

LOUISA: How do I know your art is any good? How do I know you're not just wasting your time?

MIMI: What are you talking about? You've seen my work.

LOUISA: But I don't understand it.

MIMI: It's abstract.

LOUISA: Sure, that's what every artist who heaves a can of paint at a canvas says. Apes can do that, Mimi, give them a can of paint and they're making "abstract art", too.

MIMI: I cannot believe this.

LOUISA: You have spent seven years schlepping your pictures into every dumpy gallery and store in the city and what do you have to show for it? Have you had any shows? Commissions? Has anyone even *bought* a painting?

SO WHEN YOU GET MARRIED...

MIMO: Seven years is very short time in the art world, mother. You don't just become an established artist overnight.

LOUSIA: How do you know you'll ever become one?

MIMI: I don't, but that doesn't mean I shouldn't try.

LOUISA: Take a long, hard look at your work, Maria, and then honestly ask yourself if it's really good enough to sacrifice your life for.

MIMI: I am not sacrificing my life, mother, I love what I'm doing. I'm developing, I'm growing all the time, every piece is a little better than the last one. It's not easy and it takes forever, but being an artist is like being an opera singer. You have to spend years working your tail off before you even make it to the little companies.

LOUISA: It's not the same thing at all. Singers are waiting for their physical instrument to develop, their chest and voice box. Now when I used to sing—

MIMI: When *you* used to sing?! Oh please, the only time you ever "sang" was in P.T.A. shows, so don't make out like you're some great ex-diva—

LOUISA: That's right, I never sang professionallly because unlike *you*, *I* knew the difference between fantasy and reality—

MIMI: Oh, bullshit—

LOUISA: Don't you—

MIMI: You chickened out, mother. That's what you always told me when I was little. You were scared about not being good enough so you never even tried.

LOUISA: That's not what I said—

MIMI: Goddam it, yes it is—

LOUISA: You're trying to blame me for your problems. You're irresponsible—

MIMI: No I'm not, you're jealous—

LOUISA: I most certainly am not—

MIMI: Yes you are, you're jealous because I'm not giving up like you did—

LOUISA: That's insane—

MIMI: You don't give a damn if I'm good enough, you resent the fact I'm even trying. And forget about the fact I may even be more talented

188

than you ever were—

LOUISA: I'll tell you one thing, sweetheart, I can sing a hell of a lot better than you can paint.

MIMI: You cannot you stink.

LOUISA: STINK?! Oh, you're a terrible daughter, all you ever do is hurt me.

MIMI: You're the one who's hurting me—

LOUISA: You deserve it, you're a spoiled brat who's gotten her way for too long—

MIMI: I am not, you're a nagging pain in the ass who makes my life miserable, I hate you, hate you— *(She runs out of the room. Louisa calls after her.)*

LOUISA: Double, double—fine, go, run away, don't hurt me, *kill* me. *Oy maron. Oy vay maron.* God help me, I don't know what to do anymore.

A STAR AIN'T NOTHIN' BUT A HOLE IN HEAVEN
by Judi Ann Mason
Louisiana - 1969 - Pokie (18) - Joretta (18)

Pokie: A coy high school senior who dreams of attending
college in the north.

Joretta: Pokie's best friend. Joretta is flippant, but sincere.

Pokie has been saddled with the responsibility of caring for her
elderly aunt and uncle and this threatens to interfere with her
dream of going to college. Here, Pokie is visited by Joretta, her
best friend, and the two women share their dreams for the
future.

JORETTA: Guess what, honey chile?

POKIE: What?

JORETTA: Guess.

POKIE: I can't guess. What is it? You got your letter?

JORETTA: Naw. Guess!

POKIE: Joretta I can't guess. Now tell me what it is. I ain't got long.

JORETTA: Damn! Girl you gets to be aggravating sometimes. *(In the
house, LEMUEL crosses to the chifforobe, feels around for the mail,
looks at the letters, and replaces them in order.)*

POKIE: What is it?

JORETTA: You remember when I went to the table in the cafeteria
where Sonny was sitting?

POKIE: Yeah.

JORETTA: Well, I asked him would he drive me and you to the
baccalaureate in the city...

POKIE: Uh-humm. Get to the point.

JORETTA: Well, honey chile he just called me said he would take us
on one condition.

POKIE: We pay for his gas?

JORETTA: Damn! Girl, you so un-romantic!

POKIE: What is it then?

JORETTA: He said: "Mighty right, I'll take ya'll, if you introduce me
to your foxy friend."

A STAR AIN'T NOTHIN' BUT A HOLE IN HEAVEN

POKIE: Who?

JORETTA: *You*, fool!

POKIE: Me?

JORETTA: Yeah, you!

POKIE: He want to talk to me?

JORETTA: Sho' do!

POKIE: What for?

JORETTA: I wish you would stop asking dumb questions! He must like you.

POKIE: Really?

JORETTA: Yeah. He wanted to come over here tonight...

POKIE: What? He can't come over here. *(She crosses DS.)* What did you tell him?

JORETTA: *(Crossing DS to POKIE.)* I told him to come by my house first and I would bring him over here.

POKIE: What did you do that for? You know he can't come over here.

JORETTA: How come?

POKIE: You know how my uncle is.

JORETTA: Shit, girl he ain't got to come in. Ya'll talk outside. Your uncle can't see no way. *(In the house, LEMUEL crosses to feel the face of the clock on top of the ice box.)*

POKIE: Go find him and tell him not to come! *(She is moving JORETTA toward the SL path.)*

JORETTA: Do what?

POKIE: Tell him not to come.

JORETTA: *(Breaking away from POKIE.)* Now I know you crazy!

POKIE: I won't come to the door. I'll play like I don't know him.

JORETTA: Then how we gonna get to the baccalaureate?

POKIE: *(Crossing dryness.)* I don't know. I might not be going anyway. Uncle Lemuel ain't gon let me ride with no boy.

JORETTA: Chile, have you lost your mind? Miss Davis said if we don't come to the the church, don't come to the graduation. And if we don't come to the graduation, we don't get no diploma, and if we don't get no diploma, we don't get to go to college...

A STAR AIN'T NOTHIN' BUT A HOLE IN HEAVEN

POKIE: I might not be going there either.

JORETTA: What? *(Looking upward.)* Lord, now I know this chile done lost her mind! *(Crossing to POKIE.)* What?

POKIE: Uncle Lemuel don't understand about college. *(In the house, LEMUEL moves offstage into the bedroom.)*

JORETTA: You better be trying to make him understand. Anyday now we oughta be getting them letters and we gon be packing our bags.

POKIE: We might not even get no letters.

JORETTA: We gon get them all right. Sho' as life, we getting them Just like Miss Davis say, the government feeling sorry cause Martin Luther King got killed, and they sending all the colored kids to college for free.

POKIE: They ain't sent no letters...

JORETTA: That's cause there's so many of them to send! Do you realize how many colored kids graduating from high school this year? Millions of 'em. It takes time to get to all of them.

POKIE: How we gon pay for a bus ticket way up to Ohio? We ain't got that much money.

JORETTA: *(Crossing to DSL bench at tree and sitting.)* I already made my mama promise to pay for my bus ticket up there. She running that juke-joint every weekend.

POKIE: But what about me?

JORETTA: Didn't you tell me that you get social security cause your mama and daddy dead?

POKIE: Yeah, but...

JORETTA: Then use that.

POKIE: *(Crossing to sit with JORETTA.)* But Uncle Lemuel won't give it to me.

JORETTA: Tell the folks at the social security office that he won't use the money for your education.

POKIE: I couldn't do that.

JORETTA: Do you want to go to school?

POKIE: Yeah, but...

JORETTA: I ain't never seen nobody use the word "but" so much in my life!

192

A STAR AIN'T NOTHIN' BUT A HOLE IN HEAVEN

POKIE: You just get to Sonny and tell him not to come over here.

JORETTA: I ain't. We need him.

POKIE: Don't be throwing no boy in my face just because we need him.

JORETTA: Girl, you know you like him.

POKIE: *(Rises, cross DSC.)* I don't.

JORETTA: Didn't you say he was cute?

POKIE: Yeah, I said he was cute but that don't mean I like him.

JORETTA: If you will listen long enough, I'll show you a way to let him come over here and your uncle won't even know about it... *(Rises, cross to POKIE.)* I'll tell Bernard to come over here and call me out of your house when Sonny gets to my house. I'll come outside and call you, and Sonny will be waiting over there under the tree.

POKIE: I ain't going under no tree with no boy!

JORETTA: What you scared of? He ain't gon do no more than kiss you.

POKIE: That's just it.

JORETTA: Damn, Pokie, you been kissed before!

POKIE: Not by no boy.

JORETTA: You gotta be kidding!

POKIE: No, I ain't.

JORETTA: You ain't never been kissed?

POKIE: Naw.

JORETTA: When you was talking to Billy Ray Turner, you didn't kiss him?

POKIE: Naw.

JORETTA: What about Bo Sumpter?

POKIE: No.

JORETTA: You ain't never kissed *nobody?*

POKIE: Nope, nobody.

JORETTA: Well, what do you do?

POKIE; I don't do nothing. I just see 'em at school. And anyway I wasn't really talking to them. They just got my milk carton for me in the cafeteria.

JORETTA: *(Crossing to DSL.)* Yo sho' had me fooled.

A STAR AIN'T NOTHIN' BUT A HOLE IN HEAVEN

POKIE: *(Crossing to JORETTA.)* You kiss boys?
JORETTA: All the time.
POKIE: In the mouth?
JORETTA: Where else?
POKIE: What it feel like?
JORETTA: Like a kiss.
POKIE: What's that like?
JORETTA: Meet Sonny under the tree and find out.

STEEL MAGNOLIAS
by Robert Harling
Louisiana - Present - Shelby (25) - M'Lynn (50ish)

Shelby - The prettiest girl in town
M'Lynn - Shelby's mother. Socially prominent career woman

Set in the beauty shop of Truvy Jones, Steel Magnolias follows
the intertwining lives of Truvy: her assistant, Annelle; Clairee,
the widow of the former mayor; M'Lynn; Shelby; and Ouiser,
a wealthy, curmudgeon. Here, Shelby informs her mother that
she's pregnant, even though as a severe diabetic, she knows it
is dangerous to her health.

M'LYNN: Shelby!
SHELBY: Mama? Where is everybody?
M'LYNN: I thought you weren't coming to town until after lunch.
SHELBY: We got an early start because of the traffic. We wanted to
drop in on Jackson's parents on the way down here.
M'LYNN: What a treat!
SHELBY: And you have to catch them early. On Saturdays they leave
the house at the crack of dawn to start hunting furry little creatures.
M'LYNN: You must not have visited long.
SHELBY: We didn't. I could tell they were anxious to start killing
things. We stopped by the house first. Nobody was there. Where's
Truvy?
M'LYNN: She and Annelle are out back sticking pennies in the fuse
box. They decorated that little tree and when I plugged it in all the
lights blew.
SHELBY: *(Pointing to a pair of tacky earrings.)* What are those
things?
M'LYNN: Red plastic poinsettia earrings. They are a gift from
Annelle. She has discovered the wonderful world of Arts and Crafts.
SHELBY: Are Tommy and Jonathan home yet?
M'LYNN: Yes. Jonathan got home yesterday morning. He loves his
classes. It's all he can talk about. I think the main thing architecture
school has taught him is how much he should hate his parent's house.

STEEL MAGNOLIAS

Tommy arrived last night and immediately started terrorizing your father. It's nice having the family home for Christmas.

SHELBY: Some things never change.

M'LYNN: And how are you, honey?

SHELBY: I'm so good, Mama. Just great.

M'LYNN: You're looking well. Is Jackson at the house?

SHELBY: No. You know how twitchy he gets. I sent him to look for stocking stuffers.

M'LYNN: Good thinking.

SHELBY: Uh. Jackson and I have something to tell you. We wanted to tell you when you and Daddy were together, but you're never together, so it's every man for himself. I'm pregnant.

M'LYNN: Shelby?!

SHELBY: I'm going to have a baby.

M'LYNN: I realize that.

SHELBY: Well...is that it? Is that all you're going to say?

M'LYNN: I...what do you expect me to say?

SHELBY: Something along the lines of congratulations.

M'LYNN: ...Congratulations.

SHELBY: Would it be too much to ask for a little excitement? Not too much, I wouldn't want you to break a sweat or anything.

M'LYNN: I'm in a state of shock! I didn't think...

SHELBY: In June. Oh, Mama. You have to help me plan. We're going to get a new house. Jackson and I are going house hunting next week. Jackson loves to hunt for anything.

M'LYNN: What does Jackson say about this?

SHELBY: Oh. He's very excited. He says he doesn't care whether it's a boy or girl...but I know he really wants a son so bad he can taste it. He's so cute about the whole thing. It's all he can talk about... Jackson Latcherie Junior.

M'LYNN: But does he ever listen? I mean when doctors and specialists give you advice. I know you never listen, but does he? I guess since he doesn't have to carry the baby, it doesn't really concern him.

SHELBY: Mama. Don't be mad. I couldn't bear it if you were. It's

STEEL MAGNOLIAS

Christmas.

M'LYNN: I'm not mad, Shelby. This is just...hard. I thought that... I don't know.

SHELBY: Mama. I want a child.

M'LYNN: But what about the adoption proceedings? You have filed so many applications.

SHELBY: Mama. It didn't take us long to see the handwriting on the wall. No judge is going to give a baby to someone with my medical track record. Jackson even put out some feelers about buying one.

M'LYNN: People do it all the time.

SHELBY: Listen to me. I want a child of my own. I think it would help things a lot.

M'LYNN: I see.

SHELBY: Mama. I know. I know. Don't think I haven't thought this through. You can't live a life if all you do is worry. And you worry too much. In some ways you're worrying enough for both of us. Jackson and I have given this a lot of thought.

M'LYNN: Has he really? There's a first time for everything.

SHELBY: Don't start on Jackson.

M'LYNN: Shelby. Your poor body has been through so much. Why do you deliberately want to...

SHELBY: Mama. Diabetics have healthy babies all the time.

M'LYNN: You are special. There are limits to what you can do.

SHELBY: Mama...listen. I have it all planned. I'm going to be very careful. And this time next year, I'm going to be bringing your big healthy grandbaby to the Christmas festival. No one is going to be hurt or disappointed, or even inconvenienced.

M'LYNN: Least of all Jackson, I'm sure.

SHELBY: You are jealous because you no longer have any say-so in what I do. And that drives you up the wall. You're ready to spit nails because you can't call the shots.

M'LYNN: I did not raise my daughter to talk to me this way.

SHELBY: Yes you did. Whenever any of us asked you what you wanted us to be when we grew up, what did you say?

M'LYNN; Shelby, I am not in the mood for games.

SHELBY: What did you say? Just tell me what you said. Answer me.

M'LYNN: I said all I wanted was for you to be happy.

SHELBY: O.K. The thing that would make me happy is to have a baby. If I could adopt one I would, but I can't. I'm going to have a baby. I wish you would be happy, too.

M'LYNN: I wish I... I don't know what I wish.

SHELBY: Mama. I don't know why you have to make everything so difficult. I look at having this baby as the opportunity of a lifetime. Sure, there may be some risk involved. That's true for anybody. But you get through it and life goes on. And when it's all said and done there'll be a little piece of immortality with Jackson's looks and my sense of style...I hope. Mama, please. I need your support. I would rather have thirty minutes of wonderful than a lifetime of nothing special.

UNLOCK THE DOORS
by Douglas Taylor
Small town - Present - Maddy (30's) - Ellie (40's)

Maddy - A woman who has just discovered her husband has
       been unfaithful
Ellie - Maddy's older sister

Maddy has just met her husband's illegitimate son and here tells
her sister, Ellie about the experience.

ELLIE; Well that's that—I'm set for the trip...? Maddy? Whatcha
doin'? *(Goes outside.)* Maddy? Who was that woman and what'd she
want? Maddy, ya look like you'd seen a ghost. Will you look at me—
say somethin'.

MADDY: That boy...

ELLIE: Yeah? That boy what? Gowon, that boy what?

MADDY: *(Not looking at her. From within herself)* That little boy
is... He's Ted's son. *(Crosses into kitchen)*

ELLIE: He's what... Good gawd awmighty, what are ya sayin'? *(No
response. Goes inside)* Maddy!? What in the hell do ya mean—he's
Ted's son!?

MADDY: I mean—Ted's his father.

ELLIE: How do you know that!?

MADDY: The woman said he was. She's the boy's grandmother...
(Words dwindle off)

ELLIE: That don't make it true. She could be lyin'. Did she ask for
money!?

MADDY" No, she didn't ask for anything. She wanted me to know,
so I'd do something about it. He's Ted's alright. The resemblance is
so clear—in his eyes and the mouth. He's Ted's boy. Ted visits him
every Tuesday night, and sometimes on Sunday afternoons.

ELLIE: Oh, my God—that's where he's goin' tonight. Whatcha gonna
do!?

MADDY: I don't know. It was strange. I... I had this impulse to hug
him.

ELLIE: Hug him!?

UNLOCK THE DOORS

MADDY: When I realized it was true, I wasn't angry. I just thought... This is Ted's boy, Ted's little boy and I wanted to hug him.

ELLIE: Maddy, you're batty. Always have been. Hug him!? I'd've...I'd've... *(Stops)*

MADDY: *(Looking at her)* What? What would you have done?

ELLIE: I'd've called the police!

MADDY: The police?

ELLIE: You're darn right. I'd have him arrested. Comin' around here, pretending to be your husband's son.

MADDY: He didn't have anything to do with it. Besides, he is Ted's son.

ELLIE: You're right, I guess the police are out. Well, whatcha gonna do? I'll tell ya what you're gonna do, you're gonna get a lawyer. When ya don't know what else to do—get a lawyer. And I know just the one—Harold Larsen. He's one of the best in Wawona. *(ELLIE crosses into house and straight to the telephone)* Horold'll give ya good counsel and not charge ya a penny. You remember Harold—he's the one who married Alice Cook? *(Picks up phone, dials number)* Harold's smart as a whip. He'll fix ya right up.

MADDY: Ellie, what are you doing?

ELLIE: I'm callin' your lawyer.

MADDY: I don't have a lawyer, I don't want a lawyer.

ELLIE: Ya gotta have lawyer.

MADDY; What for?

ELLIE: The divorce.

MADDY: Divorce...? Ellie, hang up—hang that phone up!

ELLIE: I won't either.

MADDY: Will you hang up!

ELLIE: Huh? What are you all upset about? *(MADDY just stares at her. ELLIE hangs up)* There's no answer anyways—probably at the courthouse. He spends more time at court than he does in bed. Maddy, ya look awful. You're goin' through hell. I kin tell. I'm very intuitive. *(MADDY's hand goes to her face, her inner tension showing)*

MADDY: I'm just trying to get my bearings. I need time to get my... bearings.

UNLOCK THE DOORS

ELLIE: Why, of course you do, honey. You're in shock. The full impact hasn't hit ya yet. But it will. It'll hit like a ton o' hay fallin' on ya. I'm surpirsed you're still on your own two feet. I'd've gone straight to bed and pulled down the shades.

MADDY: A little time's all I need—I'll be...fine...

ELLIE: Sure ya will—if ya do what I tell you. Now I want ya to sit right down here. *(She ushers MADDY to chair by table)* That's the stuff. And I'm gonna pour you one of those straight bourbons. You did it for me a while back and it fixed me up just fine. *(MADDY, sitting, clasps her hands together and presses them agianst her chin and mouth, trying to hold onto herself, emotionally)* Unhuh. It's hittin' home now, ain't it? Got a case of the shakes comin' on, ain'tcha? Well, let 'em come, don't fight it. Like Momma useta say when one of us had an upset stomach, 'Ya wanna throw up, throw up. Get it off your stomach, make ya feel better.' *(ELLIE pours bourbon into glass on table)* You don't mind usin' my glass, do ya? Ain't it funny how life is? A while back I was all messed up and you were helpin' to straighten me out. And now it's your turn and I'm pourin' for you. Life's full of surprises. You buy a ticket and take a chance. Like in the carnival. *(Stops, thinks)* Who useta say that one?

MADDY: I don't know and...I don't care... *(Sips bourbon, a lost feeling about her)*

ELLIE: I know just how you're feelin' honey, 'cause I've been through it.

MADDY: I'm going to be alright in a minute...

ELLIE: Don't count on it.

MADDY: That was the weirdest moment in my life.

ELLIE: What was?

MADDY: When I looked at the boy and saw in his face that he was Ted's. It was like a big wave washing over me, and then being under water, all sound gone—caught there underwater in time and space, me and the boy. And then...I heard someone sayin' that they were going some place, and I realized it was the woman, the boy's grandmother, sayin' she was going, standing and leaving, taking the boy with her, he looking back at me now, not afraid of me, or shy like he had been, but

201

looking right into my eyes, and then they were gone and I was alone with the knowledge that my husband had fathered a child that I didn't know existed.

ELLIE: And livin' where?

MADDY: What...? Oh—Culver Flats.

ELLIE: Right on the outskirts of your own town!? Well, I'll be a horse's rear end, if that don't take all. Your own town for how long? How old's that kid?

MADDY: He looked to be about four? Five? No, I'd say four.

ELLIE: For four years! Men. They all ought to be flogged. And you thinkin' ya had a special one. Sure he didn't want to adopt. He's got one of his own.

MADDY: No. No, Ted told me years ago he didn't want to adopt.

ELLIE: What ice does that cut? Special? A double-dealer's what you got.

MADDY: Ellie, please!

ELLIE: What? Did I say somethin' to upset you?

MADDY: *(Sipping drink)* I think I know when it happened.

ELLIE: When what happened?

MADDY: I went to that head librarians' convention in Chicago. That was about five years ago.

ELLIE: And the minute you were out of town, he went on it.

MADDY: He called me every might, sometimes twice.

ELLIE: Had a guilty conscience, betcha.

MADDY: When the convention ended, I decided to go on to my class reunion. Ted was definitely against it. I remember his trying to persuade me not to. But I thought it would be good for us to be apart, finally, for awhile, after twelve years.

ELLIE: Well, time sure proved you right. He went right out and got himself a secret child and a secret wife. *(MADDY looks up at her)* You heard me right—ya gotta gird your loins, honey, he may be married to her.

MADDY: No, oh no—Ted would never—

ELLIE: And why not?

MADDY: Well, it's against the law, for one thing.

UNLOCK THE DOORS

ELLIE: The law, the *law*! Are you tellin' me the likes of him cares about the law?

MADDY: Oh yes—he has great respect for laws and codes of con...duct... *(She stops, stares, back to a helpless feeling)*

ELLIE: Unhuh. Can't say it, can ya? Not any more, at least. Makes ya feel funny inside, don't it? Ya put your trust in 'em and they betray it.

MADDY: Ellie, I...I don't know what to do.

ELLIE: Honey, you're not gonna have to worry about a thing. I'm gonna tell ya what to do. First, ya want another drink? Okay, then— ya ready?

MADDY: Ready?

ELLIE: To pack your things.

MADDY: Pack my things!? But why...?

ELLIE: You're certainly not gonna stay in this house. With a man who's been lyin' ta ya for four years? Leadin' a two-faced life? I'm your older sister and I'm tellin' ya right this second ya ain't. So get yourself packed up.

MADDY: Where would I go? I have nowhere to go.

ELLIE: Nowhere...? We're family, aren't we? You are coming right home with me and Sue-Anne.

MADDY: I don't think I could just leave like that.

ELLIE: And why not? 'Fraid you'll give him the shock of his life? Well, he just handed you yours, or am I mistaken?

MADDY: No...you're not. Still and all... If—

ELLIE: No ifs, ands, or buts, you are comin' with me. Now shake a leg, Sue-Anne has already missed watermelon practice and she has a mess of homework to do.

MADDY: I am in shock.

ELLIE: Sure you are—you are confused and non-plussed and in no state, so bein' your older sister, I have made the decison for you.

MADDY: I suppose I could leave him a note.

ELLIE: You'll do no such thing. Let him put it together for himself. Let him come home to an empty house, his voice echoing.

MADDY: But he'd worry about me, I know he would.

203

ELLIE: That's what ya want—let him worry, let him wonder, let him swing in the breeze of uncertainty. Do him a world of good.

MADDY: You're right, I am...confused. He's such a darling little boy. I wasn't mad or jealous, or anything.

ELLIE: Will ya stop talkin' about that boy? Put him out of your mind, we don't have the time. Sue-Anne's gonna be back here any minute. You come along now—I'll help ya pack. *(She helps MADDY out of the chair and guides her upstage, as though she were a patient)* That's the ticket. We'll just go up to your room and get a few things together. You can send for the rest later.

MADDY: *(Pulling back)* Send for the rest?

ELLIE: Honey, there can be no two ways about it—you are movin' out.

MADDY: Moving out...?

ELLIE: Lock, stock, and barrel. Now come along. *(They start upstage again, into the darkness, the lights fading as they move)* You're gonna love it in Wawona. You'll have your own room with your own bath, and a big ol' sycamore tree outside your window. Won't that be nice? *(Lights continue to black as MADDY disappears into the upstage darkness, MADDY offstage, begins to scream. ELLIE rushes off, after her, the telephone begins to ring. In blackout)*

WOMAN FROM THE TOWN
by Samm-Art Williams
N. Carolina - Christmas - Laura (47) - Lila (44)

Laura Wilson - A farm woman
Lila Wilson - A real estate broker living in Brooklyn

Laura has worked her family's farm all her life and has developed a deep and reverant love for the land. When Lila, her sister, returns to Mason's Bridge from her home in New York, Laura is resentful of her success and treats her cooly. When she discovers that it is Lila's intention to take over the farm and the land, she becomes filled with rage. Here, the two confront one another.

LILA: Your dress is pretty.
LAURA: It's old, outdated and you need a shot gun to get some of these wrinkles out. I'll be delivering Christmas baskets from the church all day, so it don't matter. Too bad the old man didn't leave a will. No way he would have left you half of this place. Ain't fair you automatically own half when I'm the one who's been doing all the work all these years.
LILA: Who said that life is supposed to be fair. *(Silence.)*
LAURA: You're a rich woman, aren't you? *(Crosses into kitchen, places baskets on table and begins to get food stuff from shelf and place on table.)*
LILA: *(Crosses into kitchen stopping SR by sink.)* Suppose I told you I wanted to fix this place up. Just like new. That we could have corn in the fields come plant'n time. A new tractor. *(Crosses to above SR chair.)* Remember when we had twenty acres of tobacco? Cucumbers? Me and you running barefoot up and down cucumber rows. What about the beauty salon? I'll do it for you. *(Silence.)*
LAURA: *(SHE can't give in.)* What do you know about cucumber work? You was always sitting on the porch out of the sun...reading. I was the one working. So don't bring up no bad memories to me. I don't want your charity. I work for what I get.
LILA: Which isn't much. *(Crosses DS to kitchen stool and sits.)*

WOMAN FROM THE TOWN

LAURA: You're the one buying up all the property around here, aren't you? *(Pause. SHE is standing USL betwen UC and SL chair.)* I got nothing to give you, Lila. Look at me. What could I possibly have to give you? Sometimes, I'd be in bed... Mitchell on top of me. Trying to be tender. We'd done worked like dogs all week. Tired. Dead tired. But it was Saturday night. Our special night to be tender. Even though we'd both took baths, he still smelled like the sawmill and I still smelled like fertilizer. While we were holding on and moaning... it would flash through my mind. I'd think...Old Lila's probably laying on soft cotton sheets. Body smelling like "Evening in Paris" perfume. Her man smelling ike "Old Spice" after shave. His breath...mixture of fine champagne and Beechnut chewing gum. Cool air in your place. Me and Mitchell humping in the heat. Sweatin'. Dead tired. I'd think... Lila lives in a...

LILA: Fourth floor walk-up in Flatbush. One bedroom. You want to talk about heat? *(Rises and crosses SL above SR chair.)* Two jobs I worked. Want to talk about dead tired? Champagne?! Shit. I couldn't even afford...why the hell am I explaining myself to you? I'm not the reason things didn't work out for you. Stop using me as your reason. Find somebody else to blame. *(Crosses into parlor DSR.)*

LAURA: *(Crosses above table following and lands SL of Lila.)* I don't have nobody else to blame! And you stop using me as yours. *(Crosses above Lila landing SR of her.)* You taking your hate out on me. The two people you hate are laying out there in that grave yard. Your mama and your papa!

LILA: We are all that's left. Me and you. I'm trying to make peace with you but I will run over your ass as if you don't even exist.

LAURA: You were never a match for me and nothing's changed. Now, I haven't figured out all that's going on around here, but I got my suspicions. You'd better not be guilty of what I think you are because if you are...you'll definitely get your chance to run right over my ass. Because I'm gonna come after you girlie. Come after you real hard. *(Crosses DS of SL chair.)*

LILA: *(Crosses to below SR parlor chair.)* Before it's over, you'll be on your knees.

LAURA: We'll see. Damn it! We'll see. *(Crosses to kitchen, places food things in basket.)* Thought you come back for one thing. Damn if it don't seem like you come back for another. But I got your number. And real soon now...I'm going to call it. *(Exits kitchen, Stage Left, taking baskets with her.)*

ZOYA'S APARTMENT
by Mikhail Bulgakov
translated by Nicholas Saunders and Frank Dwyer
Moscow - 1920's - Zoya (35) - Alla (20-30)

Zoya - A widow
Alla - A beautiful woman

Zoya Denisovna Peltz will do anything to keep her Moscow apartment— including running a brothel. Here, Zoya endeavors to convince the aristocratic Alla to model for her.

ZOYA: Please sit down, Alla Vadimovna. Would you like some tea?

ALLA: No, thank you, Zoya Denisovna. *(pause)* I have come to discuss a very serious matter.

ZOYA: Yes?

ALLA: This so difficult... I know I was supposed to pay you today... This is so embarrassing, Zoya Denisovna, but I...I've had some setbacks lately...financial difficulties... I must ask you to wait... *(pause)* ...Your silence is killing me, Zoya Denisovna.

ZOYA: What can I say, Alla Vadimovna? *(A pause.)*

ALLA: Forgive me, Zoya Denisovna. I don't blame you for not answering. But I must ask you to wait two or three days, while I do everything in my power to find the money... I'm so ashamed... Goodbye, Zoya Denisovna.

ZOYA: Goodbye, Alla Vadimovna. *(ALLA goes to the door.)* You poor darling, so you've gotten yourself into a real mess...

ALLA: Zoya Denisovna, I may owe you money, but that does not give you the right to take such a familiar tone with me.

ZOYA: Oh, come on, Allachka, don't be like that! I'm nice to you and you answer coldly. That's not right! And it has nothing to do with the money. Lots of people owe money! If you had just come to me in a friendly way and said, "Things are tough right now, Zoya"...well, then, we could have figured something out together...but you came in here like the Statue of Liberty, as if you're a great lady, and I'm only a dressmaker. And if that's how I'm treated, that's how I'll respond.

ALLA: Oh, Zoya Denisovna, that's not how it was, I swear it. I just

208

felt so bad about the money that I could hardly even look at you.

ZOYA: All right, all right. Stop talking about your debt! So you have no money... Sit down. Tell honestly, as a friend: how much do you need?

ALLA: Too much. It's killing me.

ZOYA: Why do you need so much?

(A pause.)

ALLA: I want to go abroad.

ZOYA: I see. Nothing to hold you here.

ALLA: Not a thing.

ZOYA: You must have someone... I don't need to know who he is... but...can't he provide for you?

ALLA: Since the death of my husband, there has been no one, Zoya Denisovna.

ZOYA: Oh, Alla...

ALLA: It's true.

ZOYA: That's surprising. How did you manage?

ALLA: I've been selling my diamonds, but they're all gone now.

ZOYA: Three months ago, you were hoping to go to Paris. You applied for a visa. What happened?

ALLA: It was denied.

ZOYA: I can get you one.

ALLA: If you can, I'll be grateful for the rest of my life.

ZOYA: I can even help you earn some money...enough to pay off all your debts.

ALLA: How could I ever earn that kind of money in Moscow, Zoyechka?

ZOYA: Why not? There is work for you at our shop. You can be a model.

ALLA: But, Zoyechka, that doesn't pay much.

ZOYA: Not much? That depends... I'll pay you a thousand rubles a month, cancel your debt, and help you get out of the country... You'll work evenings only, every other day...

(pause)

ALLA: Every other day?... Evenings?... *(She understands.)* Quite

ZOYA'S APARTMENT

a job...

ZOYA: Just four months, till Christmas. In four months, you'll be free, out of debt, and no one, absolutely no one, will ever know that Alla worked as a model. In the spring you will see the grand boulevards of Paris. *(We hear a voice singing softly, accompanied by piano, "Let us leave the land where we have suffered so...")* Is he waiting for you there, the man you love?...

ALLA: Yes...

ZOYA: In the spring you will walk beside him, on his arm, and he will never, never know...

ALLA: What a workshop! Evenings only... What a job! Oh, Zoyka, you're a devil...and no one, no one, will ever know?

ZOYA: I swear it!

(pause)

ALLA: I'll start in three days.

ZOYA: Abracadabra! *(She flings open the wardrobe and a dazzling light reveals the Paris gowns.)* Take one, Allachka...any one you like!

211

212

213

PERMISSIONS ACKNOWLEDGMENTS